PERSONAL BEST

For my Mum, Dad and brother

Personal Best

10 lessons to help you achieve your true potential

Marc Woods

CAPSTONE

First published 2006 by
Capstone Publishing Limited (a Wiley Company)
The Atrium
Southern Gate
Chichester
West Sussex
PO19 8SQ
www.wileyeurope.com
E-mail (for orders and customer service enquires): cs-books@wiley.co.uk

CIP catalogue records for this book are available from the British Library and the US Library of Congress.

ISBN 1–84112–692–6

Typeset in Times New Roman 11/14pt by Sparks, Oxford – www.sparks.co.uk
Printed and bound in Great Britain by TJ International Ltd, Padstow, Cornwall

This book is printed on acid-free paper responsibly manufactured from sustainable forestry in which at least two trees are planted for each one used for paper production.

Substantial discounts on bulk quantities of Capstone Books are available to corporations, professional associations and other organizations.

For details telephone John Wiley & Sons on (+44) 1243-770441, fax (+44) 1243 770571 or email corporatedevelopment@wiley.co.uk.

Contents

Acknowledgements

Firstly I would like to say thank you to John Moseley and his team at Capstone for suggesting this book, and to Des Dearlove and Stuart Crainer for their advice on its structure.

For their generosity in sharing their knowledge, experience and insights, I am indebted to the contributors Jeanie Baker, Richard Cullen, Richard Davies, William Deeley, John Dunne, Professor Tim Eden, Donna Fraser, Lesley Garside, Ali Gill, Matthew Heath, Lars Humer, Kumar Kamalagharan, Georgina Lee, Giles Long, Petra Markell, Sheelagh Rodgers, Richard Shaw, David Thomas and Etienne de Villiers.

Steve Coomber's input has been absolutely invaluable. His ability to ask the right questions, make sense of my answers and understand how it would all fit together has helped turn what was a good first manuscript into what I hope the reader will consider is a quality final product.

Finally, I would like to thank my Mum, Dad and brother, without whom I would have never understood the concept of striving for my own personal best.

Preface

It is not the mountain we conquer but ourselves.
Sir Edmund Hilary

My life might have been so different.

Have you seen the film *Sliding Doors*? It's a film that explores one of those big questions in life: what if? In the film we see 'what is' and 'what might have been'. The main character is sacked from work and sets off for home via the London Underground: in one version of her life she catches a Tube train; in the other version, she misses it. An arbitrary event – the time she arrives at the train platform – sends her life in two totally different directions, and the audience gets to see how both versions play out.

Countless events shape the course of our lives, some significantly, some less so. And, as we get older, who doesn't look back on life and reflect on how things might have been? What would my life have been like if I'd passed that exam? If I'd not lost that job? If I hadn't met the person I married?

The question I always come back to is: what would my life have been like if I had not got cancer? I think I know the answer.

In my life without cancer, I make the passage from teenager to adult like any other ordinary teenager, untroubled by responsibility, unburdened by cares. Average at school, I remain average at college; I get an average job and I tick along, making do, getting by. I get a family, a house and a mortgage.

The one escape in my life is swimming. I was a good swimmer as a boy and I remain a good swimmer. A county-level swimmer – but never an *excellent* swimmer. Because that kind of excellence requires the kind of commitment that an average teenager just doesn't have. Not me, anyway. So, all in all, ordinary person, ordinary life.

Like *Sliding Doors*, the 'what is' version of my life is in stark contrast to the 'what might have been' version. Not for me the carefree years of teenage irresponsibility. Oh no. In this one I'm minding my own business when I get a swollen ankle. 'So what?', you say. Well, somehow, the swollen ankle turns into cancer. Not just any cancer either, but a nasty virulent cancer of the bone. The doctors tell me that if I don't have part of my leg amputated, I'll die. And if I do, I might still die – I'll have a 50–50 chance, instead of no chance. So, minus part of my leg, I endure six courses of chemo and survive.

The one escape in my life is swimming. A good swimmer as a boy, I become an excellent swimmer – a member of the British swimming team and a highly competitive, motivated, committed athlete. My brush with mortality, ironically, makes me realize that I am capable of much more than I ever imagined. I set myself some tough challenges and I achieve them. I knuckle down, strap myself in, and ride life's rollercoaster. I win gold, silver and bronze medals. More than that, I climb mountains, do charitable work – I even write a book. Ordinary person, extraordinary life. Well, halfway there, maybe.

Do I regret the way my life has turned out? No, not for a minute. I'm not going to say cancer is the best thing that ever happened to me. That's too glib, too easy. I wouldn't wish what I've been through on anyone else.

But having cancer has made me a better person. It's taught me to approach life in a different way. It's taught me to measure myself against my potential and not against others'. It has taught me about personal responsibility: that life is about being the best person you can be and a lot more besides.

If you are lucky, life teaches you what you don't learn at school. I've been very lucky. I've learnt some tough but invaluable lessons about life on my journey. I'd like to share those lessons with you.

Marc Woods

INTRODUCTION

My life in brief

SUMMER 1985

One Saturday, at the start of my summer holidays, my ankle becomes swollen and is painful to walk on. The most energetic things I had done was to drink a cup of tea and watch television. Over the following months I go through numerous diagnostic processes and am eventually told that, aged 16, I have a type of arthritis.

CHRISTMAS 1986

For over a year I hobble around, my left ankle gradually getting worse and starting to collapse. A new round of appointments with specialists and doctors begins. When I'm sent for a bone biopsy, I realize that whatever is happening must be pretty serious. By this time I just want to find out what is wrong. Two weeks before Christmas, I find out. I have cancer.

I have to have my leg amputated. Christmas flies by, punctuated by gatherings of concerned looking family members and more tests, this time at an oncology centre. I spend a lot of time thinking about what I will and won't be able to do in the future as an amputee.

NEW YEAR 1987

My first five-day-long chemotherapy session straddles the New Year celebrations. On the afternoon that I enter the hospital, I still have very little idea of what chemotherapy might feel like, or what it will mean to me.

Within six hours of starting the treatment, I understand the language of chemotherapy. The cancer might kill me in the long run, but the chemotherapy feels like it is trying to kill me right now.

JANUARY 1987

Amputation day approaches: 20 January 1987.

Talking to my father before the operation, I want to find something I am able to do with one leg. Swimming seems to be the answer. I was a county swimmer before and I should be able to swim with one leg. Perhaps there are competitions especially for amputees. Before I even have my operation, my father enters me for the National Swimming Championships for the Disabled the following June!

The amputation happens and I deal with it in my own way. The pain is not as all-consuming as I feared, but the phantom pains are both alarming and unpleasant. I celebrate my 18th birthday on 1 February, at the mercy of my phantom pains.

JANUARY–JUNE 1987

The chemotherapy continues to grind away at me, sapping my strength, testing my resolve.

Meanwhile, I have my artificial limb fitted.

MAY 1987

Outside the cancer ward, I'm desperate to keep hold of some level of normality. I go to see the school compete at a swimming gala.

JUNE 1987

By the time I finish my treatment, I am literally half the man I used to be. I have lost both weight and a limb.

I compete at the National Disabled Swimming Championships, which my father had entered me for six months previously. Surprisingly, I win three medals. I've come out the other end of the tunnel fighting. It's a fight I vow to carry on.

JUNE 1987 ONWARDS

Swimming becomes an even bigger focus for me once I finish my treatment. Soon I am swimming faster with one leg than I did before with two.

OCTOBER 1988

Eighteen months after finishing my chemotherapy, I'm good enough and lucky enough to represent Great Britain at the Seoul Paralympics. I win two gold medals, one silver medal and two bronze medals, a feat I consider to be pretty respectable. I have turned my life around – from the 'deathbed' to the podium – in a relatively short time and both my family and I are thrilled.

1988–2000

For the next 12 years, swimming is my priority. My father, who had taught me to swim when I was four, coached me when I went to Seoul. Now, when I go to university, I take on a new coach. I finish my degree, but it is the swimming that drives me on, and with my parents there as my number one fans, I win medals at both Barcelona and Atlanta.

OCTOBER 2000

I set my sights on competing in my fourth Games in Sydney and adding to my gold medal collection. All preparations are going well and the 4×100m freestyle relay team, which I'm part of, looks on track to win the gold at Sydney. Then, just two days before I am due to fly to Sydney, my father unexpectedly dies of a massive stroke. I cancel my flight and, along with my brother, help my mum to organize the funeral and deal with all the awful paperwork. The family is shattered. I want to be with my mum and help her. But after discussing it, we decide that I really should go to Sydney. My father would have been furious with himself if he knew he was the reason why I didn't go.

And so, the day after his funeral, I take the long, lonely flight to Sydney – one of the hardest things I have ever done. My team-mates are there for me and help me through an awful situation. The race is a memorable one. The BBC's Stuart Storey ranks it as his highlight of the games. We win the gold. It is both the best and the worst week of my life.

TODAY

Today I am no longer a competitive swimmer, but I have taken on new challenges. I have my own motivational speaking business and I also work with the Teenage Cancer Trust.

Whilst compiling my various highs and lows, I have looked at how they affected me at the time and also how they continue to affect me. Conversations with family, people with cancer and doctors have all helped me to survive some very testing situations. I have had many things taken away from me in life, but in return I have gained a respect for life itself.

ONE

Don't let life happen to you

The will to do, the soul to dare.
Sir Walter Scott

Dost thou love life? Then do not squander time,
for that is the stuff life is made of.
Benjamin Franklin

THOUGHTS ON DIAGNOSIS

We arrived back home at around 1.30am, way past my parents' bedtime if not mine. The Parent Teachers Association's annual Christmas fundraiser at my school had been a real success. Not least, because I won six out of the ten raffle prizes – a large ham from the local butcher, a bottle of Liebfraumilch, a Christmas pudding, two boxes of chocolates and of course the obligatory gift box set of Old Spice aftershave and deodorant.

The note from Dr Watkins was scribbled on a piece of paper and had been pushed through the letterbox:

Maurice,
Give me a call on 875419 whatever time you get in.
Dr Watkins

'Do you think that it's too late?' Mum said, as much to herself as to Dad. But he was already punching in the number.

'No, he knows we want to know the score as soon as possible.'

'Hello, Dr Watkins? Maurice Woods here. Right … OK … OK … we'll see you in five minutes, then.' He put the phone down and crossed the kitchen. 'He told me that I should have a stiff drink and make him a cup of tea. He's on his way round.'

Mum put the kettle on and put out the best cups and saucers on a tray. I glanced at my brother Ian, Ian at my mum. My dad was staring into thin air, his mind working at a million miles an hour as it always did.

Dr Watkins arrived looking somehow older than when I had last seen him, two weeks earlier. He took a seat and launched straight into what he had to tell us.

'I know you are all eager to find out the results from the biopsy. I have been chasing Mr Evans for news, but he was keen to get a second opinion.' His hands holding the cup and saucer shook. Not just a little tremble: it was so pronounced, it looked like a hammy actor trying to do 'nervous'. 'But it has been confirmed now. You have an oesteosarcoma, or bone cancer. You will have to have your leg amputated below the knee and six sessions of chemotherapy.'

Tears welled up in Dad's eyes.

'What if I don't want to have my leg amputated?' I asked.

'Then you'll die,' was the instant reply. 'Bone cancer is a very virulent type of cancer and this course of treatment has been proven to give the best prognosis. You will have one course of chemotherapy first, then your amputation, and then the other five bouts of chemotherapy.'

I left the room. In the kitchen I leant against the units and began to cry.

'Don't cry, mate,' my brother said as he came in.

'Why me?'

'You'll be all right.'

And then I thought about it. What would my friends and peers think? What would I think if it was one of them that had cancer? I'd probably be mildly concerned, but it wouldn't stop me from living. It wouldn't stop me deliberating over what I would have for my tea.

'You're right, I will be all right,' I said. 'People aren't going to be that upset for me, so I won't let it upset me. What happens to me isn't going to stop them living, so I won't let it stop me from living.'

I'm not sure how much logic there was in that thought, especially given the circumstances, but at the time it seemed to make me feel a whole lot better. I didn't know if I had six months, six years or sixty years left to live – but I did know that from this moment on, I was going to live my life to the full.

Until that moment, I had been the typical teenager, just happy to let life wash over me. But this was a pivotal moment in my life. It was the proverbial 'kick up the arse' and it made me realize that I no longer wanted life to just happen to me. From that point on, I wanted to take control of my own destiny as best I could.

DON'T LET LIFE HAPPEN TO YOU

Before I was catapulted into the world of cancer, I was like most of the people I meet – I let life happen to me. From day to day, life impacted on me and I did very little to affect it.

As humans, we have a predisposition to die. Every cell, from the moment it forms, is programmed to die. Every skin cell, every hair cell, every blood cell has a spell of life that is planned, before it self-destructs. Scientists call it 'apoptosis': programmed cell death.

But sometimes, something goes wrong within the cell. Somehow the DNA gets damaged and the cell changes its attitude. A cancer cell is born and, given the chance, a cancer cell loves to live. It stops doing the tasks that its mother cell performed and then begins to divide, replicating itself with a view to hanging around for as long as possible. It doesn't self-destruct. Cancer cells are strong – they have character. All cancer cells are trying to do is live. The only way you can get rid of them is by poisoning (or irradiating) them into sub-mission. That's what the chemotherapy does. Chemotherapy encourages the cancer cell to commit suicide.

People talk of cancer being sinister. They whisper about it under their breath as if the cells are listening. All cancer is trying to do is live, but it is life at all costs, life until its host is dead.

It was only when I came face to face with these cells, so to speak, and their passion for life, that I decided to be passionate about life myself. I was going to have an effect on my life and not just let life happen to me. It is amazing what it takes for some people, and I am including myself in this, to realize that life is a do-it-yourself thing.

Many people need a push in life before they actually start living. They cite near-death experiences, or the loss of a loved one, as events that have made them re-evaluate their life and how they want to live it. Such things can force a period of self-reflection so thorough that it affects the very nature of how an individual wants to spend the rest of their days. They make a decision about how they want to actively approach life. But what about the people who haven't suddenly been faced with their own mortality, or suffered a terrible loss or shock? Those people who are living life passively? I certainly don't recommend searching out such experiences; instead, let's try and learn from those who have been there.

Extraordinary lives

History is full of examples of people who have grasped life with both hands; people who have got up off of their backsides, got on and achieved great things; people who have been proactive rather than reactive.

We all know about the great leaders, for example Sir Winston Churchill, or humanitarians, such as Mother Teresa. Their achievements are world famous. But these are not the only people who have seized the day and attacked life with vigour. Root around a little in the archives of history and it doesn't take long to discover that there are countless less well-known tales of ordinary people living extraordinary lives.

In 1961, Jean Nidetch was an ordinary middle-aged housewife living in Queens, New York. Like many other women, she struggled to keep her weight down.

Nidetch could have muddled on, fighting the good fight against fat and trying out the latest diet fads, but – where keeping off those extra pounds was concerned – getting nowhere fast. Instead, she decided to take action. She invited six friends over to her apartment to discuss their common predicament. The next time they met, she handed out copies of a slimming plan she found in an obesity clinic run by the New York City Department of Health.

Within two months, that small group of friends had expanded to 40 or so people. Nidetch's waistline, however, like many others in the group, decreased substantially. Initially she weighed in at 193lb (13 stone, 11lb) but was soon down to 134lbs (9 stone, 8lb). The group dieting thing obviously worked.

Soon they were holding meetings at other people's houses. In 1963, the group having long outgrown her apartment, Nidetch hired a theatre in Queens. She was expecting about 50 people to come along – 400 showed up. Realizing the whole thing was getting a little to large for her to handle alone, Nidetch found a business partner, Al Lippert, and founded Weight Watchers.

Nidetch ran the company for 15 years before finally selling to the Heinz corporation in 1978. She remained a consultant with the brand she created until 1998.

George Mercer Dawson didn't get the greatest start in life. Born in Pictou, Novia Scotia in 1849, he contracted tuberculosis of the spine when he was a boy. It left him with a hunched back and restricted his growth development to the equivalent of a twelve-year-old child.

But Dawson wasn't about to rail at his misfortune, or languish at home an invalid. Initially he was too ill to go to school, so he was educated at home. But, after a lengthy period of recovery and recuperation, he went to study part-time at McGill University in Canada and later attended the Royal School of Mines in England.

Dawson returned to Canada in 1873, aged 24, when he was appointed geologist and botanist to Her Majesty's British North America Boundary Commission. For the next 20 or so years, Dawson travelled thousands of miles on geological surveys. He travelled from western Ontario to the Rocky Mountains, through British Columbia, and the Yukon, to the Bering Sea.

Little by little, he meticulously mapped out large tracts of Canada, covering the mountains, lakes and valleys by horse, railway, steamboat, canoe and even on foot. The physical challenges were immense, yet Dawson conquered them.

He was appointed as Palaeontologist and Chief Geologist of the Geological Survey of Canada (GSC) and later became a director. In 1896, he was elected President of the Geological Society of America.

As well as his scientific achievements, Dawson left a historical legacy in the archive of photos taken on his journeys. They are photographs documenting the birth of modern Canada, and the extraordinary career of a man who lived life with a flourish.

On a summer's day in July 1944, a young African-American woman got on a Greyhound bus heading for Baltimore. The

27-year-old mother of two was on her way to see a doctor. She sat near the back of the bus in the section reserved for 'coloured' people.

When she was asked to give up her seat for a white couple she refused, telling the women sitting next to her – one of whom was holding a baby – to stay put. The bus driver headed for the nearest sheriff's office, pulled up outside the jailhouse and called a sheriff onto the bus, who attempted to arrest her. At which point she tore up the ticket and fought with the deputy who dragged her off the bus.

She later recalled in an interview with *The Washington Post*: 'He touched me. That's when I kicked him in a very bad place. He hobbled off, and another one came on. He was trying to put his hands on me to get me off. I was going to bite him, but he was dirty, so I clawed him instead. I ripped his shirt.'

She was subsequently jailed for resisting arrest and breaking segregation laws.

That women wasn't Rosa Parks, whom some of you might have heard of. It was a woman called Irene Brown, ten years before Parks stepped onto that bus in Alabama that would make her so famous.

In court, Brown pleaded not guilty to breaking the segregation laws but was found guilty and fined $10. At that point most of us, with centuries of history and the weight of the US judicial system against us, would have probably paid the fine. Not Brown, though.

She appealed and her lawyers pursued the case to the Supreme Court which, in a landmark ruling, overturned the segregation laws in interstate transport situations. Although the Southern states refused to follow the ruling in *Irene Morgan v. Virginia*, Brown's actions led to a series of freedom rides. In the first, 18 black and white members of the Congress of Racial Equality (CORE) travelled throughout the South on buses, whites at the back, blacks at the front, on a 'journey of reconciliation'. Many ended up working on a chain gang for 90 days.

Irene Brown went on to live a life that would have been impossible had it not been for her actions and those of others in the US civil rights movement. She won a scholarship in a radio competition and studied for a first degree in communications – aged 68. She got her masters degree in urban studies – aged 73. Before this, she ran her own childcare business in Queens, New York.

The problem for most of us is that doing things at 90% of maximum effort is easy. The extra 10% may be disproportionately difficult, but it is that little bit extra that makes us exceptional. The first step is to decide that this is a journey that you want to take. It is not a quick or easy process: it may well take far longer then getting the first 90% right. It fact, it may even take you the rest of your life.

Just my luck

I was lucky: something happened to me to make me re-evaluate my life. I am one of many people who have had a major life crisis. It can be a serious illness, losing your job, losing someone close to you, a narrow miss, an accident, or an event that stops you in your tracks for a moment – psychologically, physically, or both.

Better still, for me, it happened when I was young enough for it to make a difference – although it can still galvanize you into action if it happens later on in life.

And, perhaps even more importantly, I was lucky enough to be the kind of person who took the positive, rather than the negative, from a situation. Not everyone would view such a major life crisis as positive.

Psychology professor Richard Wiseman, author of *The Luck Factor,* conducted research into people's attitude towards luck. A broad range of people took part in the study: at the two extremes, some participants considered themselves to be very lucky, others very unlucky, with a range of people falling somewhere in between. As part of the study, Wiseman proposed a scenario to the 400 participants and recorded the various responses.

The scenario was as follows:

You walk into a bank to cash a cheque and, as you are standing in the queue, someone decides to rob the bank. In the confusion, a gun is fired and you are shot in the leg and wounded. But you survive. What would be your response?

One set of people responded with answers such as 'Why is it always me?', 'I'm always in the wrong place at the wrong time' and 'Life is so unfair'.

Others replied along the lines of 'Well, it could have been a lot worse; we could all have been killed' or 'I am lucky to be alive'; and, in extreme cases, 'Wow, that's lucky – I could write a book about it!'

Obviously the scenario was the same for everyone, so it is only the individual's attitude towards the scenario that varied. No doubt you know which camp you fall into – the people who considered themselves to be generally unlucky in life; or those who believe luck is with them.

Personally, I feel that we make our own luck through the choices we make. We are all capable of positive and negative thoughts and attitudes; the important thing is to let the positive side control the negative and not vice versa.

Bitterness

We don't have time to be bitter about events – it's far better to use them as a catalyst to spur us on. It's not always easy, but perhaps we should follow the example of Nelson Mandela. If anyone has a right to be bitter, it is Nelson Mandela. Twenty-seven years enduring the brutal prison regime on Robben Island, a place Mandela described as 'the harshest, most iron-fisted outpost in the South African penal system'. Incarcerated for struggling against injustice and subsequently exonerated by the actions of later generations.

Nelson Mandela was awarded the Nobel Peace Prize in December 1993, along with F.W. de Klerk, the man who ordered his release and then helped to run the government with him, for 'their work for the peaceful termination of the apartheid regime, and for laying the foundations for a new, democratic South Africa'.

At the award ceremony, the chairman of the Norwegian Nobel Committee noted: 'many people have remarked on the apparent lack of bitterness that characterizes Mandela's conduct since he was released from prison. He himself has said that perhaps he would have harboured bitter thoughts if he had not had a job to do.'

Would Mandela have achieved what he has in life if he had wallowed in bitterness and hatred following 27 years in prison? Obviously not, and millions of people should thank him for his strength.

Not everyone, however, has the benefit of a life-changing event to spur them on. So what about these people? If that's you, then you may well be thinking, 'Do I really need to re-evaluate the way I live my life?' It's a fair question. Why should you bother?

Perhaps it is worth considering a few statistics.

- The average American spends 52 days a year watching television. That means a 70-year-old will have spent over ten years of their life watching television. Even if you exclude the first ten years, that is still 8.5 years.[1]
- In the UK, the average commute to work is 45 minutes per day. Over a year, that is the equivalent of 34 eight-hour working days. Over a working lifetime from 18 to retirement at 65, that is about four years and three months of your life spent travelling to and from work.[2]
- According to the World Toilet Organization – yes, such a thing exists – the average person spends about three years of their life on the toilet.
- If we live to 70 and assume that we get an average of seven hours' sleep a night, we will have spent the equivalent of a little over 20 years, 24/7, asleep.
- In China, people from Beijing spend one hour and 42 minutes eating daily. That's 25 days a year, and just short of five years 24/7 if they live to 70.
- The average person over 50 will have spent five years waiting in queues and one year looking for lost items.

In other words, just taking account of these few activities, someone who lives to 70 will have spent 47½ of those years, eating, sleeping, going to the toilet, travelling to and from work, watching television, waiting in queues and searching for lost items.

When you look at life in this way it makes you realize how little time we actually spend doing the things that matter to us. What value, for example, do you place on watching television or commuting to work, or sleeping, compared with doing things with your family, travelling or spending time with friends?

---

[1] TV turn off network/AC Neilsen
[2] RAC Foundation report 2003

If you throw work into the equation, especially if you don't enjoy your work, then there is very little time left for you. Most people don't stop and think about things like this, or only very rarely – they are too busy getting through life, living from day to day. Because of my illness, I was forced to confront the way I lived my life and how I wanted to live it.

Surely, though, it would be better if it didn't take a major life crisis to make you think seriously about what you want from life and how you want to live it. That's one of the reasons why I wrote this book: I found out the hard way, but hopefully you can take a short-cut.

BE PROACTIVE

My recovery has given me a second chance. Others don't get one and start from a worse position. I can't do anything about yesterday but I sure can about tomorrow. 'Tomorrow is the first day of the rest of your life'.

Richard Shaw
Teenage Cancer Trust trustee

LET'S GET IT ON

This book contains anecdotes and insights from my life experiences, and details of how I turned a major life crisis into a positive life-affirming outcome. It is not meant to be prescriptive: my illness and my subsequent experiences as a competitive swimmer have taught me some useful lessons about life. Take from them what you will.

If you follow some or all of them, I strongly believe that they will help you achieve your personal best in whatever it is you want to do.

If you are going to take on the challenge, you will need some weapons in your armoury, some ideas about how you can change your life for the better. In the rest of the book I will write about:

Being the best you can be

Few of us appreciate what we are truly capable of. No matter what your starting point is, you can do more than you think: more physically, more mentally.

Constant goal setting

There's little point in setting out on a journey if you don't know where you are going. People do better with goals than without them, provided those goals are well chosen.

Motivation

It's the 'why' of what we do. It's the reason we get from A to B. No motivation, no goals achieved. The obvious motivation is that attractive carrot – money. But money isn't necessarily the best motivator. You need much more than financial reward for motivation if you are going to improve your personal best.

Teamwork

We all work in teams of one sort or another. Don't believe me? Well if you are not in a formal team at work, you are probably in an informal one. Outside of work there is family life, even if it is a team of two. If you live and work alone, there's your social network. And if none of the above applies, you are probably not reading this book but stranded on a desert island.

Communication

Effective communication is at the heart of excellent personal performance. Communication isn't just about talking, though – much of personal communication, for example, is non-verbal. And listening is one of the most important communications skills you can master.

Adversity

The path to doing well is rarely an easy one; there will always be setbacks and it pays to know how to deal with them. Stress is a big factor in modern life. It is hard to reach your true potential if stress is holding you back. Luckily, there are ways of combating stress that really work.

Role models

We don't arrive in the world with an innate knowledge of how best to live our lives. We need guidance from somewhere. This is where role models come in. But not just any role model, not the conventional pop, movie and sports stars. Role models are all around us, we just need to find the right ones. Well-chosen role models and mentors help us help ourselves to get better.

Prejudice

Prejudice does not just eat away at individuals and society, it impairs performance. Prejudice prevents you from finding out what people are really like and thus from developing useful networks and alliances. It gives you a misshapen worldview.

Learn how not to perpetuate prejudice or let it affect your life.

The edge

If we can get a fair advantage, why not take it? It so often separates the excellent from the nearly excellent. There are many techniques that can help boost personal performance. Some may work for you, some may not – try them and see.

As you finish this chapter, ask yourself if you want to live life actively. Hopefully, the answer will be 'yes'. Once you have decided to make the journey, you must commit to being the best you can be at that very moment in time. Not tomorrow, next week or next year, but right here and now.

TWO

The best you can be

The difference between what we do and what we are capable of doing would suffice to solve most of the world's problems.
Mahatma Gandhi

The battles that count aren't the ones for gold medals. The struggles within yourself – the invisible, inevitable battles inside all of us – that's where it's at.
Jesse Owens

LEARNING TO WALK

At the age of 18, I learnt to walk again. It is a strange thing to have to do for a second time. Of course I had mastered it once when I was a toddler, but then, the whole thing was automatic. The second time around was a different proposition.

The first part of the process was to be given an artificial leg. Limb fitters look like a cross between a doctor and a janitor. They wear white coats, but instead of stethoscopes and thermometers, they carry wrenches, screwdrivers and Allen keys.

I remember the limb fitter walking in my direction, my new leg swinging in his hand.

'Here is your pylon,' he said in matter-of-fact way.

My first thought was: 'I wish he would call it a leg'. After all, it looked a bit like a leg, with a plastic foot at one end and a socket and strap at the other. 'Pylon' sounds mechanical. 'Leg' sounds human. I wanted to feel human.

The fitter was around retirement age, with an attitude that matched the decoration of the fitting room – drab, tired and disappointed.

'Put this stump sock on,' he said, passing it to me. Then he pulled the socket lining out of the leg and pushed it onto my stump with a force that made my chair slide back along the tiled floor.

'Now push the lining back into the pylon.' I did as I was told.

'That's quite tight,' I said, my stump still unaccustomed to any rough treatment.

'It's meant to be,' he replied curtly. 'Do the strap up.'

The strap went around the bottom of my thigh, just above my knee.

'Now walk in between the two bars.'

I made my way to the parallel bars hobbling like an old lady with bunions after a day's shopping. By now I could race around on my crutches. So I wasn't expecting my mobility to be *reduced* when I got my leg.

'Let's check the alignment,' he said.

'This is quite painful.'

'Well, what do you expect? I can't make you a real one.'

Now I ask you. What is the minimum amount of compassion you should expect from someone working in the National Health Service? A reassuring smile from a maternity nurse during childbirth? A psychotherapist asking your name? A surgeon using a scalpel and not a plastic spoon? This guy definitely didn't meet the minimum requirements.

'I just thought you should know that it is uncomfortable.'

'Well it's going to be, isn't it? Take it home with you, but don't wear it until you get a call from the physiotherapy department. They'll tell you how to use it.'

And that was it. End of appointment. He put my leg – uncomfortable or not, it was still my leg and not a pylon – into a large brown paper bag and gave it to my Mum, who was waiting at reception.

ORDINARY PEOPLE, EXTRAORDINARY LIVES

Comparing the personal best times of 18-year-old athlete Oscar Pistorius with the Olympic record books throws up some interesting facts. Had he raced the 100m in 1906, his time of 11.16 seconds would have won the gold medal; in 1920, his 200m time of 21.83 would have again won the gold; and if he had competed in 1928, his 47.34 for the 400m would have also seen him at the top of the podium.

Perhaps you think this is not that impressive as we are now in the 21st century, but I have omitted to mention one detail: Oscar runs with two artificial legs. Pistorius was born without fibulae and several bones in his feet, so surgeons amputated both feet before his first birthday. He has become known as the fastest man with no legs.

100%

The fitting of my artificial limb was a dispiriting experience, but it taught me an important lesson. As far as I was concerned, the limb fitter chose not to be the best he could be at his job.

If the harsh news that I had cancer forced me to reassess my life and decide to live it to the full, then there was no way I was going to make a second-rate job of it. I decided, then and there, that whatever I did, I was going to do it to the best of my ability. I would be the best I could be.

When I got home, I started to practise walking. To begin with, I walked along still using my crutches and barely putting any weight on my new artificial leg. As I walked along the pavement outside my house, I carefully measured my stride length, comparing my left leg with my right. I made sure that each leg did the same thing. Once I had perfected this, I started to put more weight through the artificial leg.

This process went on for weeks. To begin with, people would say 'Hey, Marc, you're walking well – I can hardly tell you have one leg.'

Most people in my position would be happy with this. My reply was 'What do you mean "*hardly* tell"? What am I doing wrong?'

At the time, we lived in a large bungalow with several windows. I would walk up and down the driveway, looking at my reflection in the glass. Sometimes I would see my Mum inside and I would get her to listen to the sounds of my footsteps. If she heard a limp I would try and eradicate it.

There were times when I overdid it and made my stump so sore I couldn't wear my leg for several days. Eventually, though, I grew used to it. After two months, I was excellent at walking again. You couldn't tell my artificial leg from my real one. It was hard work, but putting the extra effort in has paid off in numerous ways, not least in being able to do something that I love. In recent years, I have trekked and climbed in various places around the world, including the Andes and the Himalayas.

In life, many of us settle for second best. We end up, either actively or passively, committing ourselves less than 100% to a task or to our lives, whether it is completing a project at work, being a parent, sticking to a diet or keeping our New Year's resolutions – whatever it may be.

If you are someone who gives 90%, but not 100%, you may take some comfort from the fact that there are understandable reasons why people find it difficult to put in the extra effort, either mentally or physically, to be better than average.

OUTSIDE THE COMFORT ZONE

Driving through the gates of the Royal Military Academy at Sandhurst was the first, very small part of a year-long journey that constantly pushed me out of my comfort zone.

The British Army Commissioning Course led me to discover who I really was and what I was capable of achieving. It certainly gave me the foundation for my military career, but I have also applied the skills learnt on the course to my career after leaving the army.

Having had very limited contact with the military previously, I was already on the 'back foot' in comparison to those cadets who were seasoned OTC and TA attendees. Something new was thrown at me just about every day; some of these were physically challenging and some mentally challenging. The course pushes you to your physical and mental limits and beyond. Never before would I believe I could walk for three whole days carrying a load of kit and with only four hours' sleep. And yet I did it and so much more.

Lesley Garside
Operations Director, Northgate HR

Why do we settle for less?

There are many reasons why people settle for average as opposed to exceptional. Here are just a few that affected me – I suspect many of you will be familiar with some of them:

- fear of failure;
- fear of the unknown;
- fear of being in the spotlight; and
- lack of motivation and disillusionment.

Fear of failure

No one likes to fail – society places a premium on winning. Darwinism, natural selection, survival of the fittest – as humans, we are genetically primed for survival. It is an instinct that follows us through life, through work and often through leisure.

Failure is stigmatized and frowned upon. Before the middle of the 19th century, for example, individuals who were declared bankrupt were subject to the death penalty. In the US, they were nailed by the ear to a post and flogged. Fortunately for many entrepreneurs, bankruptcy policy is a bit more enlightened today, although it still has a stigma attached to it.

People soon learn that the best way of avoiding failure is by not risking it. By sticking to activities that we know we are capable of, we can carry on our lives safe in the knowledge that we are unlikely to be branded a failure. It's the comfort zone that we so often hear about.

And it doesn't have to be a major challenge, such as climbing Mount Everest or singing in front of a crowd of 100,000 at the Glastonbury Festival. It can be small everyday things: whether to wear that slightly daring dress, whether to take on a project at work, whether to give a presentation, whether to write a book. Every day, we make countless decisions influenced by our comfort zone. Even people that you might assume have no fear of failure still operate within a comfort zone. It's all relative.

Take the world of climbing. Not, you might think, a sport for the faint-hearted. Yet within the climbing world, there are varying degrees of danger.

The safest form of climbing is sport climbing, where beginners are securely fastened to a top rope. The rope is fastened above and below the climber. If the climber falls, the rope stops them falling more then a couple of feet.

The next stage in a climber's development is to learn to lead a climb. Here, as the individual progresses up the rock face, they clip themselves onto existing bolts in the rock face set along the climbing route. As they climb from one bolt to the next, the potential fall is the distance between the climber and the last bolt. So they are at their most vulnerable just before clipping on to the next bolt. The further the distance they have climbed to that bolt, the further they could fall before being brought to a nasty halt by the bolt below.

Climbers who are very competent with a top rope will often struggle to adjust to leading. In their case, failure has a very tangible result of bad bruising and broken limbs. For most of us, the potential failure is less physical, but no less painful. Whether it hurts our bank balance or just our ego, it still hurts.

Fear of unknown

In a similar way that people fear failure, they also fear the unknown. Although some people thrive on chaos most prefer stability. As Peter Gabriel once sang: 'I know what I like, and I like what I know.'[1] We like to understand the world around us. We like order. Consequently, we fear the unknown. This is why so many people dislike change. Yet this aversion to change and fear of the unknown holds us back both as individuals and as a society.

6 May 1954 was in important day both in athletics and human achievement. For years, running a mile in less than

---

[1] 'I Know What I Like (In Your Wardrobe)' from *Selling England by the Pound*. Performed by Genesis. Written by Banks/Collins/Gabriel/Hackett/Rutherford.

four minutes was considered not just impossible but, according to the leading medics of the time, dangerous to the health of anyone who even attempted it.

Yet on a windy day in May, Roger Bannister crossed the finish line in a time of 3 minutes, 59.4 seconds. In doing so, he broke both a world record and a psychological barrier.

Australian John Landy, one of the fastest middle distance runners of the time, had attempted to break the four-minute mile many times before. Within 46 days of the breakthrough, Landy smashed Bannister's record, running the mile in 3:57.9. By the end of 1957, 16 runners had logged sub-four-minute miles.

We have to tackle the unknown to make progress. If some individuals had not been willing to enter into the unknown and embrace change, the world would be a different place: Columbus wouldn't have discovered America, man wouldn't have stepped on the moon, Everest would remain unconquered and there would be no open-heart surgery.

Fear of being in the spotlight

The Sunday Times once asked 3000 Americans what their greatest fear was. Top of the list with 41% of the vote came 'speaking in front of a group', some way ahead of the 19% who said 'dying'.

What is it about public speaking that turns grown adults into a physical and mental wreck? The fear of being in the spotlight can root a person to the spot. Everything seems back to front. Palms get damp, mouths dry. The heart races, but the brain slows down. The throat constricts and the bowels … and all before you utter a word.

I speak from experience. On 24 March 2003, I was attending a concert organized by the Teenage Cancer Trust at the Royal

Albert Hall. The band performing was Coldplay; 20 minutes before they were due on stage, I was asked if I wouldn't mind popping out and speaking to the 5000 fans and encourage them to continue supporting the charity in the future.

Did I mind stepping out in front of 5000 people who were impatient for the main event to start, and without any preparation? Well, yes I did mind, or at least it made me break out into a sweat, but I did it anyway. And I'm glad I did.

Humans are social creatures. Many of us do not enjoy being the focus of attention. We like to melt into the crowd. We like to be the same rather than different.

Lack of motivation and disillusionment

Before I started my cancer journey, I was rarely motivated to do anything. I would be happy to blame others for my short-comings but unwilling to do anything about them.

I felt that I didn't have the help that I needed from some of my teachers. 'No-one has told me how to revise' was one of my favourite comments. It was true – no-one had – but I did nothing to find out for myself. I was disillusioned with the whole academic process because I didn't know what job I wanted and I couldn't see how many of my classes were going to help me in the future.

Motivation is a very important issue and an integral part of achieving your personal best. It is covered in more depth in Chapter 4.

HIDDEN DEPTHS

The truth is that we are all capable of much more than we believe we are. This is true both physically and mentally. It's like the story of the mother lifting a vehicle to free her child.

Absurd though it sounds, such tales are not as crazy as they might seem.

Results obtained from individuals under hypnosis suggest that such prodigious feats of strength may be possible by many people. In one case, the average strength of the grip of three men increased by 40% from 101lb to 142lb when they were hypnotized.[2]

Hypnosis has also been used as an analgesic aid in surgical operations. In the 19th century John Elliotson, Professor of Practical Medicine at University College, London, practised surgery using hypnotism as a substitute for anaesthesia. It was also used during the Second World War when conventional anaesthesia wasn't available, and it is even used today by some surgeons.

A friend of mine, Dave Thomas, is a great example of someone unlocking hidden powers. Dave was working as a fireman when he had a 'eureka moment'. He saw a programme about memorizing packs of cards. Something clicked and he decided to get the book, the video and whatever else he could lay his hands on.

Within two weeks, he could memorize a pack of cards. Within three months, he could memorize 1000 digits. In 1998, Dave, who was never that great at school – he was expelled – did something that would have astounded his teachers.

'May I have a large container of coffee right now?' is a mnemonic for the first few digits of Pi – the figure that represents the ratio of the circumference to the diameter of a circle. The number of letters in each word is the same as a digit of Pi. Pi starts 3.14159265358979323846264338327 95 and goes on and on … and on. In September 2002, Professor Yasumasa Kanada at the

---

[2] Robin Waterfield, *Hidden Depths: The Story of Hypnosis*, Macmillan, 2002.

University of Tokyo, with the help of a Hitachi supercomputer, calculated the value of Pi to 1,240 billion decimal places.

In 1998, Dave broke a record that had stood in the Guinness Book of Records for 18 years.

The list of people who have memorized Pi is a long one. The list of those who have memorized over 1000 digits is somewhat shorter – 80 or so. The list of those who have memorized over 20,000 contains just six names – and Dave Thomas is one of them.

In 1998, Dave recited 22,500 digits of Pi. He didn't do it the easy way, either – if there is one. On his first attempt, he got to 18,000 digits and then got one wrong. I don't know how you would have reacted, but I know how I would have. And it wouldn't have been to do what Dave did – start again. Dave eventually broke the record and is ranked fifth in the all-time world ranking.

So Dave turned out to be a supreme mental athlete. The analogy he likes to use is that it is a bit like running a marathon. Most of us could run a marathon. Dave's 18 stone but he could run a marathon, given enough time, training, practice and nutrition. But not everybody, and definitely not Dave, is going to do it in 2 hours and 30 minutes. No. Dave is the 2 hours 30 minutes in memory.

So Dave discovered he was capable of much more than he ever imagined and, as he often reminds me, most of us only use a tiny fraction – less than 10% – of our brain. Which means we are all capable of much more.

The truth is that most of us don't realize what we are truly capable of. Not unless we are lucky enough to stumble across something that helps unlock our talents; or we are forced into a situation where we have to find out. Had it not been for cancer, I would probably never have discovered how good a swimmer I could be.

Waving not drowning

The day after I had my stitches removed, I was off to the local swimming pool.

In my early teens I was a good swimmer, swimming for my school, local team and county. I loved competing, but never took training that seriously. By the time I reached the important exams at school, I had all but given it up. But then came the cancer, the chemo and the amputation. Everything changed. Suddenly I had a strong desire to get back to the pool. To get back to something that I knew I could do, despite only having one leg. If I was good enough to race for my county (but too lazy to be any better), I figured having one leg wouldn't prevent me from swimming reasonably well.

Arriving at the pool I gently slid into the water, holding my stump high, paranoid about hitting it on the bottom. The water was soothing. It felt odd to begin with, unbalanced, but I concentrated on using my arms rather than my legs, and gradually it began to feel very natural. The most natural thing I had done for a long while.

I had no idea how my life was going to change, but I was sure I was going to be able to swim. And this time it was going to be different. I wanted to be the best I could be at swimming. Average wasn't good enough any more.

In the break between my fifth and sixth chemotherapy course, my Dad took me to the local swimming pool to watch my school swimming team compete in a gala. I got my first swimming badge in the same pool when I was four years old. Now it didn't feel so big and intimidating. By this time I'd been swimming a few times since the amputation and always at this pool. It was almost a home away from home.

But that day I wasn't swimming, so instead of going through the changing rooms onto the poolside to race with the others, Dad and I made our way upstairs to the spectators' gallery.

I loved everything about going to the pool: the smell of the chlorine, the sound of the water, the noise from the spectators. Sitting in the gallery and watching the swimmers warm up was strange, though. I wanted to be in the water.

Mr Lucas, the teacher in charge of swimming, waved to me and came over. Dad and I went to the front of the gallery to lean over and talk to him.

'Hello Marc,' he said. 'How are you?'

'Good, thanks – but I'd rather be swimming than watching.'

Dad was under strict instructions from Mum not to let me swim. She was worried I was getting run down and that swimming would just make matters worse. The last chemotherapy course had been delayed because my white blood count was too low. And I only had three more days to go before my final chemotherapy session.

'You can if you want to,' said Mr Lucas.

Mr Lucas looked at Dad. Dad looked at me.

'Well, it's up to you.'

'Great! Let's go!'

I left my leg and my clothes with dad and made my way onto the poolside using my crutches. I chatted with friends and watched the other races. Just being there, alongside the rest of the school team, was exciting. As the competition heated up, so did my nerves. There was a good crowd, 300 spectators, plus 150 swimmers. With everyone packed into the building, the atmosphere was electric.

Then it was time for my race – the 100m backstroke over three lengths of the pool. Mr Lucas walked to the start with me and left me sitting on the chair at the end of my lane.

As I hopped a couple of times to the edge of the pool, there was a sudden silence. Plenty of people knew I had been unwell; some did a double take when they spotted me earlier in the evening and saw how thin I was and how ill I looked. As I jumped into the water in my ill-fitting borrowed goggles and trunks, and my newly acquired stump, everyone was staring at me.

I put my right foot on the wall, gripped the starting block with my hands and balanced myself with my left knee on the wall. Up until then, any exercise I had done over the previous few months had been recreational and remedial. Now I was taking a big risk. Right there in front of all those people. Although I'd decided that I wanted to become a great swimmer, rather than a mediocre one, I had no idea whether I was capable of competing – I just had a foolish hunch that things might turn out OK. On top of it all, I risked making myself ill. Maybe even too ill to take my chemo in three days' time.

Before I had time to think about whether it was the best thing to do, the starter said: 'Take your marks' and fired his gun. After years of practice, my response to the gun was involuntary. Given the circumstances, my start was surprisingly good. I was just in the lead. And then we came to the turn.

I had no idea whether I could still turn properly with one leg. More to the point, I was worried about banging my stump against the side. I knew how painful that would be. So when it came to the first turn I took it very carefully, almost in slow motion.

By the time I was back into my stroke, I could see other swimmers had caught me. The next turn had to be a lot smoother and a lot faster. I put the fear to the back of my mind and whipped round as fast as I could. No pain. When I came up, I was ahead. From there to the finish, I just pushed as hard as I could and hoped.

I touched the wall and quickly glanced both ways. As the water emptied out of my ears, I heard everyone cheering. Mr Lucas was jumping up and down with my crutches in his hand. I had won my first race back. It felt great.

WHAT DOES IT TAKE?

Is it possible to be exceptional at everything? Of course it isn't. Not even Leonardo da Vinci was brilliant at everything – although he came close – but it is possible to aim to be exceptional all of the time, to try to be the best you can be.

Through experience, and talking to other people who are the best in their field, I have discovered there are a number of steps you should take on the way to being the best you can be:

- sweat the small stuff;
- are you sitting comfortably?;
- making sacrifices;
- set your own standards;
- mental strength and determination;
- set yourself specific goals; and
- avoid being distracted by apathetic people.

Sweat the small stuff

The simplest thing to do is to focus on the small things. If you can get all the small things right, then the overall result is excellence. There is a common phrase 'don't sweat the small stuff' but in this instance it is the aiming to get the small stuff right that leads to the overall goal being a success.[3]

---

[3] Carlson, Richard, *Don't Sweat the Small Stuff*, Hyperion, 1997.

Gary Player once said: 'The harder I practise, the luckier I get.' What he meant was the more he practised, the less luck came into it. He was very good at getting the small things right and aiming to be exceptional.

As my swimming career progressed and evolved, I began to focus more on the 100m freestyle and less on the distance events. To be a valuable part of the relay team, I had to become a better sprinter. I could have shrugged my shoulders and said 'I am what I am' and 'You can't teach an old dog new tricks'. But instead, I deconstructed my technique and rebuilt it. I spent months altering the pitch of my hand at the front of my stroke by little more than a couple of degrees. Tiny difference, big results.

Are you sitting comfortably?

A big step along the way is to make the conscious decision to push your own personal boundaries. Anybody who is successful has stepped out of their safety zone into a place where they aren't entirely comfortable.

In terms of your own aspirations, take some time to think about those aspects that you are comfortable with and those you are unsure of. This uncertainty indicates where the fringes of your comfort zones are. For example, a salesperson may aspire to progress within the structure of their business from their current position as a sales representative to a manager of a sales team and then on to become a sales director. Confident with their general communication skills, the thought of presenting to the entire business at the company conference might well be outside of their comfort zone and fill them with dread.

Once the boundaries have been acknowledged it is possible to start doing something about pushing them and stepping outside of them – even removing them altogether.

PUSHING THE BOUNDARIES

Starting a business in the music industry, I got funding and advice from the Prince's Youth Business Trust and was given an estimated three to twelve months as a lifespan of the business. Against these odds and completely scared of failure, I had the determination and tenacity to continue.

Kumar Kamalagharan
MD of Fruit Pie Music

Personal sacrifice

I'm not suggesting that being exceptional is easy, even for those lucky enough to be blessed with incredible natural ability. What the smiling faces on the podium don't reveal is the sacrifice that has helped them get there.

Here is an example of my training schedule from January 2000 as I prepared to go to the Sydney Paralympics.

4.40am	Alarm call		
5.00–5.30am	Pre-pool session	Emphasis	Core control exercises Injury prevention – shoulder stability exercises Abdominal exercises
5.30–7.30am	Swimming session	Emphasis	Step test, anaerobic threshold set Swim down protocol

		Race warm-up	400m freestyle 200m backstroke 200m freestyle 300m kick descending each 100m 300m freestyle 200m freestyle at step 3 pace 200m freestyle at step 1 pace 200m easy freestyle
		Step test	7×200m descending to maximum effort Measuring heart rate, stroke count, blood lactate and perceived rate of exertion each 200m
		Anaerobic threshold set	16 x 100m on 1 minute 40 seconds
		Swim down protocol	200m easy, 400m @ 40 BBM 4×100m @ 50 BBM with bursts of strong kicking 200 @ 40 BBM, 2×100 @ 50 BBM
		Total distance	6400m
12.30–2.00pm	Gym workout	Emphasis	Strength Power
		Basic gym work	1 warm-up set, then 3×8 for each of the following: lat pull downs, squats, pull ups, bench press, shoulder press cleans, straight arm pull downs, triceps extensions, bicep curls.
		Medicine ball	3 × 10 for each of the following: sit up and throw, standing slams, standing throw, overhead throw
4.00–4.30pm	Pre-pool session	Emphasis	Core control exercises Injury prevention – shoulder stability exercises

4.30–6.30pm	Swimming session	Emphasis	Power rack ATP/CP – sprint work Cord assist/resist	
		Warm up	Anaerobic threshold kick set 400m freestyle 24×50m freestyle (6 steady swim, 6 build with race finish, 6 with a blind turn, 6 race start)	
		Anaerobic threshold kick	200m 30 seconds rest 2×100m 20 seconds rest 4×50 15 seconds rest	} ×2
		Skills	16×25 15 seconds rest – technique work	
		Power/speed	10 15m attached to 20kg on the power rack 100m easy freestyle 2×25m sprint and 25m easy	
		Recovery	2×50 cord work 200m easy freestyle	} ×2
		Swim down	2×200 pull negative split 4×50 pull hypoxic breathing 200m easy freestyle	} ×2
		Total distance swum	5700m	
		Total distance swum in day	12,100m	

For me, training was one of the toughest aspects of being the best. I had to train, but to train the way I did meant personal sacrifice. Sometimes it was hard on my family; it was certainly hard on my girlfriends. It's rarely possible to give 100% without making some sacrifices, whether it is time away from the family because of work or giving up something you enjoy doing to focus on the task in hand. There will inevitably be personal sacrifice. Only you will know, in each instance, if it is a sacrifice you are prepared to make.

PERSONAL SACRIFICE

Many successful people make sacrifices to achieve greater success. You need to evaluate the importance of these sacrifices against your set goals and be clear about who is making the sacrifice. After a successful spell building the Disney brand in Europe, I had an opportunity to work in Los Angeles – but this would have meant relocating to California at a time when my family had become established and settled in the UK. Although it was a fantastic business opportunity, it was not, on balance, a sacrifice I was prepared to make, as I believed my family – and not I – would have suffered most.

Etienne de Villiers
Chairman of the ATP

Set your own standards

If you don't think you are up to the challenge, take some comfort from the example of Tiger Woods. Even if you are not a fan of golf, you have probably heard of him. He is possibly the greatest player ever to pick up a golf club.

In 1999, aged 23, Woods won a record £4 million on the Professional Golfers' Association (PGA) tour. Out of 21 PGA tournament starts, he won eight and finished in the top ten 16 times. He was a member of the US team that fought back on the final day to beat Europe and reclaim the Ryder Cup.

The following year, he won both the US and British Open championships. In 2001, he won five PGA tournaments, becoming PGA Player of the Year for the third consecutive year. Even more impressively, he won the Masters tournament in the same year and became the first golfer in history to be reigning champion while holding all four major tournaments simultaneously: the Masters, the US Open, the British Open and the PGA. In 2003 he won the US Masters again.

After this kind of success, most people would think all they had to do was more of the same, and more trophies would inevitably follow. Not Woods. He split with his coach. He then set about reassessing his whole game. He tried different clubs, different golf balls, altered his swing and got a new coach.

Why? Because although he was an excellent golfer already, he felt he could be better. He strives constantly to be the best player he can. And so he sacrificed two years of his golfing career, and life, to improve his game even more.

Woods explained the way he went about improving his game to the *Los Angeles Daily News*: 'I had a bunch of things I needed to work on and try to solidify. Each and every day was a task to try to figure out what I needed to work on that particular day. But as the year progressed, the checklist got shorter and shorter. And consequently, results started improving.'

If Woods had been focusing on what everyone else was doing, would he have done that? It's unlikely. Woods sets his own standards. So can you. It is crucial to measure yourself against your own potential – not against the limitations of others.

Mental strength and determination

Aiming to be exceptional all of the time is going to be very difficult. Part of the challenge will be to stay determined and motivated.

John Landy, as you now know, was the second man to break the four-minute mile. Perhaps he is best remembered, though, for his role in the 1500m final at the 1956 Olympic Games in Melbourne. Landy and fellow Australian Ron Clarke were leading with two laps to go when Clarke caught the heel of another runner moving through to the lead and fell. Landy and the rest of the field leapt over Clarke, but Landy then turned back to help him to his feet. Incredibly, Landy then continued to run and made up what was a huge deficit to claim the bronze medal.

Over the years of striving and struggling to be the best I can be, my will power and determination can be distilled into one sentence:

'Am I being true to myself?'

If I can answer that with a yes, then I know I am on the right track.

Set yourself specific goals

Motivation is nothing without a goal. Once you have decided that you are going to try and be exceptional, select some specific targets. To begin with, you should select goals that are not too challenging. In business they call this picking the low-hanging fruit, or going for the easy wins. If you succeed early on, it will inspire you with confidence.

A year before the trials for the Barcelona Paralympics, I looked ahead at what I wanted to achieve in 1992. My goals were to get a good result in my degree and a medal at the

Barcelona Games, but there was a potential problem. I knew I would have to study for my finals, complete my dissertation and qualify for Barcelona all within a few stress-filled weeks.

I broke my goals down into achievable sections. Every day, I would aim for a balance between academic study and training. To try and reduce the pressure on myself, I obtained a full list of all my academic obligations for that year and I began to plan my work. In October, I started on assignments that weren't due until the following May and so I continued, working through the list in reverse order. Occasionally I would go to the top of the list to do some impending items. By February, I met myself in the middle – I had completed all of my work for the year, much to the disgust of some of my peers. But critically, it meant that my time was then freed up just when I needed to focus on qualifying for Barcelona. And I justified the planning and the hard work by achieving both my goals.

TAKE YOUR MARKS

As we come to the end of this chapter, let me ask you a question: If you were the best in the world at your chosen career, would you think about deconstructing what you do and rebuild your game if you thought it would help you improve? Hopefully, the answer is yes. Sure, constantly striving to be excellent is a challenge – but the rewards really are worth it.

THREE

Constant goal-setting

Man is a goal-seeking animal. His life only has meaning if he is reaching out and striving for his goals.
Aristotle

You are never too old to set another goal or to dream a new dream.
C.S. Lewis

The big secret in life is that there is no big secret. Whatever your goal, you can get there if you're willing to work.
Oprah Winfrey

AROUND THE NEXT CORNER

I have always tried to have a goal to work towards in my life. I might not be the fastest, but I normally get there in the end. During my swimming career, one goal rolled into another: Paralympic Games ... European Championships ... World Championships ... European Championships ... Paralympic Games – and so on for five Paralympic cycles.

But I have set myself other challenges – goals away from the swimming pool. Goals that are now more important to me. One is to enjoy my motivational speaking, the lifestyle that it offers me and the impact it has on others. Another is to support the Teenage Cancer Trust.

The Teenage Cancer Trust is fortunate to have some generous friends. Not all give money, some give something equally valuable – time. Giving time can make a huge difference. Roger Daltrey, the lead singer of The Who, shares my passion for the Teenage Cancer Trust. He says, with good reason in my opinion, that quality treatment is a right, not a privilege. With the influence he has within the music industry, for one week each year he is able to persuade an incredible list of stars to perform at the Royal Albert Hall.

My involvement varies each year. I have been asked to speak to the audience about the work of the charity and announce bands such as Oasis. On other occasions I have helped to encourage the people in the corporate hospitality boxes to lend their support in the future.

By far the most enjoyable experience for me, however, is when I am directly involved with the people who, more than anyone, appreciate the significance of the event – young people with cancer. We invite teenage cancer patients to the concerts.

For them it is a once-in-a-lifetime opportunity to meet some of their idols. I remember a young boy who had just finished his course of chemotherapy saying to me as he was leaving the hall: 'That's the first time I have felt normal for over a year.'

You can't place a value on providing an uplifting experience for people who are enduring an intense physical and emotional ordeal. In this instance, my role is to try and make sure that the patients have the best possible time at the concerts. We get everybody together in the afternoon, which is both a chance to hear some of the soundchecks and to meet other teenagers going through similar experiences. The teenagers swap stories with each other and discuss details of how they try to cope.

Each night is exceptional, but the highlight is usually when the patients meet the stars. Often both groups are nervous; the patients because they are meeting a big star, and the artists because they are meeting some very ill individuals.

A sizeable amount of money is always raised and the profile the Teenage Cancer Trust gets in the national media helps to generate awareness of the issues of the people that we try to help.

ORDINARY PEOPLE, EXTRAORDINARY LIVES

At 43, Jean-Dominique Bauby lived a life that many might have envied. He was editor of France's *Elle* magazine, with a promising career ahead of him. Then, in 1995, he suffered a stroke. The stroke left Bauby in a condition known as 'locked-in syndrome': the brain worked fine, it just couldn't communicate with the body. The only muscle that Bauby was able to control was his left eyelid.

There was virtually no hope of making a full or even partial recovery. Finding himself in such a desperate situation, Bauby decided to write a book about his plight. With the help of a frequency-ordered alphabet and a companion, he dictated prose by blinking each time his companion pointed at the correct letter. In this incredibly painstaking way, Bauby wrote *The Diving-bell and the Butterfly*. The butterfly is Bauby's imagination trapped inside the diving bell of the body. At over 130 pages, the book represents an incredible feat. Bauby died in 1997 shortly after publication.

One door closes ...

Retirement can be stressful. A study by the psychologists Jungmeen Kim and Phyllis Moen at Cornell University found that a significant proportion of men who retired while their partners were still working suffered from low morale and depression.[1] The men that were happiest were those that continued to work if they wanted to and who had a partner who remained at home.

Erik Erikson was a leading psychoanalyst who taught at Harvard University and developed a seven-stage model of life.[2] The seventh stage is the period of middle adulthood, from around 35 through to the late 50s. It is described in terms of a struggle between generativity and stagnation.

---

[1] Kim, J. & Moen, P. 'Couples' work status and psychological well-being in older adults', Session 4639, 23 August 1999, American Psychological Association.

[2] http://www.ship.edu/~cgboeree/erikson.html

By 'generativity', Erikson meant caring for others: having and raising children, and also teaching, writing, the arts and sciences, inventing, and other activities that satisfy a need to be needed.

'Stagnation' speaks for itself. It is about self-absorption, not caring for others or finding time for yourself or others, and withdrawing from social situations.

In all stages of our lives, it is important to have something to aim for, something that keeps us going. Whoever we are and from whatever walk of life we come from, we need something to work towards. When you have reached the end of a particular focus in your life and you have either achieved your goal or failed, it is imperative to replace it with another challenge. If not, you are left with a void.

It is often said that athletes struggle to come to terms with their retirement from sport. Indeed, even if they continue competing, many athletes struggle with the sense of anti-climax in the period directly after a major competition. Some even become clinically depressed.

My last competitive swimming race took place in Athens. After the highs of winning the gold medal in the 4×100m freestyle relay, I had a reality check in the heats of the 100m backstroke. With a rotator cuff muscle tear only partially repaired I was not competitive, and just missed out on a place in the final. As I climbed out of the pool, it dawned on me that this was it … my last moment as an international athlete and a competitor. The end of 17 years on the British swimming team.

I took my time as I made my way along the poolside, trying to savour every moment, listening to the crowd and looking at the pool until I was eventually ushered away by an official. I had a brief conversation with a journalist in the mixed zone and then walked away … an ex-athlete.

When I reached the end of my swimming career, I felt a sense of emptiness. I know it sounds ridiculous, but having achieved my goals, I was at a momentary loss at what to do. However, as I said at the start of this book, I vowed after surviving cancer not to let life happen to me but to take it on wholeheartedly. All I needed to do then was find another challenge or two.

GOAL-SETTING

Goal-setting is essential because without it, how would you know where you were going? If you set goals, you are able to appreciate where you are going and move on to establish the route to getting there.

I always picture goals as a road, and along that road I place markers or milestones that, when met, demonstrate that I am making progress. I also attach timelines to the markers so that I can check progress against this plan. Maybe I need to amend the plan along the way, but I always ensure that the goal remains achievable.

Lesley Garside
Operations Director, HR Northgate

Serial goal setters

Ray Kroc was a fairly average guy. It was the 1950s, and Kroc had worked most of his life travelling the US as a milkshake mixer salesman. He was a good salesman but, at 52, he was beginning to contemplate a pleasant retirement. Until, that is, he wandered into a small restaurant in San Bernardino, California in 1954.

The burger restaurant was the culinary equivalent of Ford's assembly line. There was a limited menu, five milkshake machines producing 40 milkshakes at a time, plastic utensils and paper napkins, and a burger served at a competitive price within 60 seconds. For Kroc, it was a revelation, so he persuaded the two young brothers to license their name to him – the brothers were Dick and Mac McDonald.

Kroc applied himself to his new goal with gusto. He opened his first restaurant in Des Plaines, Illinois in 1955. He even had a laboratory for creating the perfect French fry. It was a struggle and he almost went bankrupt early on. In 1960, his restaurants earned $75 million but produced profits of just $139,000. In 1961, Kroc bought out the McDonalds brothers for $2.7million. When Kroc took McDonalds public in 1965, he was $3 million richer. His fast food empire expanded across the world and by the 1970s, Kroc had turned his $2.7 million into a $500 million fortune.

To Kroc, however, the money wasn't the main goal. The goal was making McDonalds the best it could be. His focus was on maintaining the standards of the restaurant chain. He did allow himself a few indulgences, however – such as buying the San Diego Padres baseball team. Later in his life, when people would remark on his good fortune, Kroc would reply: 'Luck is a dividend of sweat. The more you sweat, the luckier you get.'

Sexually abused as a young child, an unsettled childhood spent at different times with her grandmother, mother and father, almost sent to a home for juvenile delinquents – it doesn't read like a recipe for adult success.

All credit to Oprah Winfrey, then, that she managed to build such a successful and groundbreaking career in radio and television from such unpromising beginnings. Her lucky break came at 16 when, as the first black girl to win a national beauty contest, she was invited on a tour of a local radio station to pick up her prize. She was talent-spotted and asked to read the news after school. Setting her sights high, she became a reporter on the Nashville radio station WVOL at the same time as enrolling at Tennessee State University on a performing arts course.

She became a news anchor at WTVF-TV in Nashville – the first Afro-American to do so. Next came her own morning chat show on AM Chicago, going head-to-head with Phil Donahue, America's top-rated talk show. She also received an Oscar nomination for best supporting actress in Steven Spielberg's *The Color Purple*. Winfrey's next goal was to control her own destiny. In 1988, she formed a production company Harpo Productions, spent $20 million on a production facility and became the third woman (after Mary Pickford and Lucille Ball) to own a major production studio.

Despite setbacks and a constant personal battle with her weight, Winfrey remains one of the most popular television personalities in the US. One of her latest challenges has been her self-avowed aim to get the US television-watching public reading. The book club segment of her show has taken the publishing world by storm. Her recommendation has the power to sell hundreds of thousands of copies of a book.

These are just two more well-known examples of people who have continued to push the boundaries. Open to opportunity when one goal was completed, another filled its place.

Why is it important to have goals?

Originally, I wasn't aware that what I was doing was goal-setting. Looking back, it is clear that I had quite distinct goals and clearly defined steps on the way to achieving them.

When coping with my cancer treatment, I allowed the natural progression of each chemotherapy treatment to act as a marker. Each time I finished a week of treatment, it was a small success on the way to completing the entire course.

As a swimmer I had major goals, such as winning gold medals. But I only managed to achieve a major goal by having multiple goals to reinforce the ultimate one. For example, to win the gold medal, I had to compete well as often as I could. To do that, I had to train as well as possible every time I went to the pool. To achieve that, I had to eat well and rest sufficiently. Each major goal is broken down into smaller more readily achievable targets. It is like a house of cards. The ultimate goal is to place the final pair of cards at the very top. But without placing the cards beneath properly, the house will never be finished.

GOAL-SETTING

Is goal-setting important in life? Absolutely! I set goals every day. I set short-, mid- and long-term goals every year, and I do my utmost to achieve them. If I don't achieve them in that year, I work harder and identify why I didn't, but I never change the goal to suit my current ability.

Donna Fraser
Olympic athlete

GOAL BASICS

Before setting goals, there are some basics that are useful to know. Goals can be categorized by type. Two main types are performance and outcome goals.

For performance goals, the focus is on the way in which an outcome is achieved – the performance. The person setting the goal retains as much control over the goal as possible. In a running race, for example, this might mean running with the correct technique. You may not win the race, but you will achieve your goal and hopefully improve your performance. If you are cooking a meal it may mean getting the best ingredients and following the recipe and cooking instructions to the letter. The people eating the meal may not enjoy it for many reasons outside of your control, but you will have produced a good end result. If you are trying to lose weight, your goal might be to eat a certain number of calories a week, use the right food groups and do a set amount of exercise.

Outcome goals are where the focus is on the eventual outcome. My goal was to win gold medals. However, I had less control over this goal than over a performance goal, such as swimming ten sessions a week in practice. I might swim a personal best and yet not win any medal at all.

You might find it surprising, but sports science has shown that better overall results can be achieved by setting performance goals.

Another way of looking at goals is in terms of timescales. Short-term and long-term goals are self-explanatory. It is advisable to have both. Short-term goals provide impetus for day-to-day action. Long-term goals provide help us get through tough times and provide us with direction.

SMART GOALS

SMART, as in SMART goals, is an acronym that aids the goal-setting process. There is a slight problem in that various versions exist, so the letters stand for different attributes. Here is one common version:

- **S**pecific – goals should not be so vague as to be meaningless. They should specify what will be achieved.
- **M**easurable – it should be possible to measure progress towards goals.
- **A**chievable – the goals must be achievable, not fantastical. (Sometimes listed as action oriented/actionable.)
- **R**ealistic – is it a realistic goal given the resources, environment, etc.? (Sometimes listed as reasonable/relevant.)
- **T**ime – are the timescales clear? (Sometimes listed as trackable.)

Challenges come in all sizes

People have a strange notion of charity. Most people want to live in some kind of nirvana but not everyone wants to pay for it and so, in the UK at least, charity steps in to fill some of the gaps. Yet when some people talk of doing charity work, they almost snigger it under their breath.

I have my own – and, to the reader, hopefully obvious – reasons for supporting the Teenage Cancer Trust. So throwing myself into the Trust's work and supporting them to the best of my ability has become a new goal, to some extent replacing the drive to compete and win medals. I never thought that anything could replace the feeling of competing in a swimming championship and the buzz of achieving my goal by winning, but I was wrong. No matter what your goal is, or how fulfilling it is to accomplish it, there is always something else that you can do that will fill that space.

I know what it's like to lie in a hospital bed next to people that you feel you have nothing in common with. So I understand the benefits of bringing together teenagers with cancer for their treatment, creating the most positive environment possible for them.

I am passionate about helping to provide the quality of care that they deserve. A true benefit of winning a gold medal is seeing the pleasure it brings to others – I see no point in winning a medal, then locking it away in a safe. The achievement of winning the medal is nothing to what can be achieved for others after it has been placed around your neck. To me, it is selfish to hide it away from others, and doesn't tap into the power such an object has.

I sometimes spend time at the children's hospitals in Sheffield and Manchester. A nine-year-old boy called Jonathan once watched a video of me swimming and decided that I was his hero. One of the nurses on the unit contacted me and I happily went to visit him. Jonathan had a bone cancer similar to the one that I had suffered from. He had been through one lot of treatment already and was told he was in remission, but he knew something wasn't right with his leg when his foot kept slipping off his scooter.

His leg was due to be amputated in a couple of weeks, but even then his prognosis didn't look good. He was fantastic and just sat with my medal around his neck and smiled at me the whole time. His parents couldn't buy that kind of reaction, and it would never have happened with my medal safely tucked away behind locked doors.

Whenever I meet someone like Jonathan, I try and give them something to help them remain positive. I often used to give them the medals that I would win at the National Swimming Championships. Unfortunately, I didn't win as many as I needed to give out.

How do we choose appropriate goals?

Setting a goal can be a very personal thing, but here are some basic guidelines to help you in forming yours.

It is possible to split your life into the different sections that are important to you. There are no rules as to how you do this, but below is how I have decided to do it:

- family and home life;
- friends and social life;
- physical and health;
- financial and career;
- cultural and education;
- spiritual and ethical; and
- public service.

The ultimate challenge is to have a clear goal that has a positive impact in each of these areas, or to have separate goals within each of these sections.

It is imperative that none of your goals contradict each other. For example, you may have a financial goal that also fits well with your plans for your family, but if the way you intend to acquire this income contradicts your personal ethical beliefs, the system will collapse.

My loosely compiled goal rules are as follows:

- Ensure the positive aspect of the goal is the focus. For example, when I was swimming, I would always try and focus on the correct technique to adopt – not the one I should avoid.
- Create incremental goals on the pathway to your larger goal.

- Wherever possible, measure how successful you are being. Create markers on your journey towards your goal and celebrate those successes.
- Set goals that you have as much control over as possible
- Find a balance between a challenging goal and a realistic goal. If an unrealistic goal is set, then motivation will soon wane.

Before setting your goal in stone, take some time to think about how you are going to achieve it. Ask yourself some questions:

- Do I have all the information I need?
- What obstacles am I likely to face?
- Am I being blinded by my own ambition?
- What skills do I need to acquire to achieve this?
- Who can help me to achieve my goal?
- Is there a better way of doing things?
- What will success look like?
- When am I going to re-evaluate this goal?

GOALS AND PLANS

'A goal without a "plan" is just a dream' – so I always set a goal and have an action plan, measures (so I can see how I am doing) and a timescale. Simple, but I can set numerous measures that get me towards the end goal and enjoy many successes and fewer failures.

Richard Shaw
Teenage Cancer Trust trustee

Evaluating and re-evaluating

Choosing a goal or goals is only half the battle. As well as goals, you will need an action plan, some performance or outcome standards and a way of measuring against them. You will also need some way of monitoring progress.

There are bound to be setbacks. Later in the book, we will look at different ways of coping with them.

Put all this together and you have the drivers for improving whatever it is you want to improve; for achieving whatever it is you want to achieve.

Changing tack

Goals aren't set in stone. There may be times when a goal becomes outdated or outmoded, or is just no longer useful to your life. There's nothing wrong in changing or modifying your goals. In fact, it is a good thing, as it ensures that they are always relevant, that you are continually assessing your progress towards those goals, and that you are flexible enough to cope with the shift in direction.

For most of us, failing to modify or reassess goals means we waste valuable time pursuing goals that are no longer valid. For some people, however, it is the difference between life and death.

The great explorer Ernest Shackleton set out for the South Pole on 9 October 1908. It was the culmination of a voyage of discovery that had set out from England in August 1907. Shackleton and his three fellow explorers, Frank Wild, Dr Eric Marshall and Lieutenant Jameson Adams, didn't get off to a great start when a pack pony kicked one of them, exposing the bone.

What followed was a grim drama played out in the bleak, icy landscape of the Antarctic at temperatures below –40°C. They constantly had to rescue each other from crevasses and suffered from biting hunger, which forced them to shoot and eat three of the four ponies that carried their equipment (Socks, the last pony, fell down a crevasse). They ate pony maize. Adams had a tooth extracted without special tools or pain killers.

Slowly approaching their goal, the weather got worse. A blizzard on 30 December prevented then from travelling more than four miles. Weak and at risk of frostbite, they had reached the limits of their endurance.

On 2 January, Shackleton wrote: 'I cannot think of failure yet. I must look at the matter sensibly and consider the lives of those who are with me … man can only do his best.' There were blizzards from the 4th until the 8th of the month, the last two days of which they were unable to travel. Only 97 miles from the pole, Shackleton reassessed his goals and took the decision to return. His decision saved his own life and the lives of his companions.

To his wife, Shackleton wrote: 'I thought, dear, that you would rather have a live ass than a dead lion.'[3]

Robert Falcon Scott, another legendary polar explorer, was not so fortunate. Faced with equally difficult decisions to make in January 1912, Scott and his exploration party pushed on past Shackleton's mark in an attempt to be the first to reach the South Pole. As history notes, it was possibly the wrong decision, as none of the party survived to tell the tale. All perished on the return journey, having reached the pole only to find Norwegian Roald Amundsen had beaten them to it by a matter of a few weeks.

---

[3] Shackleton's expedition is recounted in his book *The Heart of the Antarctic: Being the Story of the British Antarctic Expedition 1907–1909*, William Heinemann, 1909.

What is important to you?

Ultimately, the goals you set have to be important to you. You may set worthy goals, but if they do not have some personal resonance, you are far less likely to achieve them. After reflecting on what it is that you want to do and achieve, make sure that it is true to who you are and not just an attempt to please someone else.

In 2001, along with my good friend William Deeley, I set out to climb Mount Cotopaxi in Ecuador, the world's highest active volcano at 5697m. We hoped to raise tens of thousands of pounds for the Teenage Cancer Trust.

It was another challenge I had set myself. Fighting cancer had been a challenge. Winning my gold medals was a challenge. Helping the Teenage Cancer Trust continues to be a challenge.

After two days in Ecuador, we both became very ill with food poisoning and ended up in a hospital in Quito. I lay in bed, hooked up to a drip, my body convulsing with a massive fever, and wished I had never set foot in Ecuador. The trip, as far as I was concerned, was over; I could barely walk the three metres to the toilet.

It took three days for us to be fit enough to get discharged from hospital and whilst we had spent the majority of time wishing we were back home, a sense of obligation crept up on us. We had to at least try and achieve what we had set out to do. And so, after sorting out our kit, we got a jeep to take us to the base of Cotopaxi.

We ate some plain boiled rice and snatched a few hours of sleep before leaving the refuge at one in the morning while the ice on the glacier was hard and therefore easier to walk on with our crampons.

With my energy tank almost empty, the climb became the hardest physical test I had ever done. I settled into a rhythm of placing my ice pick and plodding onwards and upwards. After seven hours, Will and I both reached the top of the volcano. Tears streamed down my face. It sounds clichéed to say it now, but I felt I had done it for those teenagers who never make it out of the cancer hospitals and never get the chance to do it themselves. I couldn't have done it without them.

FOUR

Why am I doing this?

People who are unable to motivate themselves
must be content with mediocrity, no matter
how impressive their other talents.
Andrew Carnegie

Money was never a big motivation for me,
except as a way to keep score. The real excitement
is playing the game.
Donald Trump

GETTING OUT OF BED

January and February are two of the toughest months for any British swimmer. When your alarm wakes you in the morning and you head out into the biting cold, it is pitch black outside. When you leave the pool after completing your evening work-out, it is pitch black again, still cold and probably raining. The excitement and tension of summer competition seems like a mirage in the distance.

During the early months of 1995, the prospect of competing at the Atlanta Paralympics was still over eighteen months away. I tried to keep my ultimate goal, winning a gold medal in Atlanta, at the front of my mind, but sometimes it was almost impossible. The winter months were taking their toll, the mental and physical pressure dragging me down. Getting out of my warm bed and heading into the cold for morning training became increasingly difficult. I was fast approaching the limits of my motivation.

I tried to make things as easy as I could for myself. It was a sad sight. I prepared everything the night before: packed my swimming kit in my rucksack, laid out my clothes on the floor, in the order I put them on, even put the toothpaste on my toothbrush ready for the morning. All so I could have a few more precious seconds in bed.

Eventually I reached breaking point. It was a Friday morning in late January and I had just turned off my alarm. The flashing display read 4.40am. My apartment was freezing. Outside the wind whined, and the rain smashed against my bedroom window. Already that week I had swum over 50,000 metres. If I had been swimming the English Channel at its narrowest point, I would have been well on the way back by now. I was exhausted. So tired I was physically shaking. There was no way I was going training. So I crawled back under my duvet, said 'Stuff training', and went back to sleep.

OK, I didn't really. I wanted to. Instead, I sat on the edge of my bed with my duvet draped around my shoulders staring at my clothes on the floor. I mulled over the pros and cons of not going to the pool. Would it matter if I missed one training session? I had trained flat out every day that week. Most swimmers missed workouts occasionally; it's a punishing sport to train for.

Then I thought about what would happen if I didn't go. The other swimmers would just about register my absence. They wouldn't care that much. There would, after all, be more room in the pool. One person would care, though – my coach.

Doug Campbell was the British record holder for the 200m backstroke in the early '80s. As a retired swimmer with a couple of decades of coaching behind him, his belt now fastened a few notches wider than it used to. He was a mountain of a man, with an unfeasibly broad back on a solid frame that seemed better suited to contact sports than swimming. And he was still unbelievably committed to his sport.

So I wouldn't be there, but my coach would, and he'd be disappointed. I could lie back down in my bed, sleep some more, and wake up feeling physically better. Psychologically, though, I'd feel worse. I couldn't let my coach down. He was investing time in me. We were a team, both working towards that gold medal in Atlanta. We had a mutual respect for each other. Did I really want to risk damaging that for the sake of a couple of extra hours in bed?

When I started my car and looked at the clock on the dashboard, I was just two minutes later than normal. Two minutes is all that process took. Just a brief moment, but in hindsight, some of the most valuable minutes I have ever spent.

THIRD PARTY MOTIVATION

Third party motivation was powerful for me. It was not until I told friends that I was going to do something that I would actually do it. If I kept it to myself, then nothing was achieved – as soon as others hounded me about something that I'd claimed I would do, I would get to it and generally achieve it.

Matt Heath
Yachtsman

About motivation

We have all been there. Who hasn't woken up on a dreary morning, for example, and thought how nice it would be not to bother going into work? There are few of us who haven't taken a 'sickie'.

So why don't we do it every day? The reason is that most of us are motivated to go to work. The motivation may be different: for some it will be the fear of being sacked, for others the need to make money, for others still, the social aspects of work. But, without motivation, we wouldn't do anything.

Motivation has some fancy science to explain it (see *The science of appliance*, pages 71–2) and define it. At its most basic, however, motivation is the reason for behaving a certain way – for taking a certain course of action.

When you are faced with a challenge, whether it is something that you have chosen, or something that others placed in front of you, you need to be motivated. If your goal is where you are going, your destination and motivation are the reasons for getting there. Or, more importantly, the *reasons*.

In simple terms, if the goal is cooking dinner, the motivation, at its most basic, might be avoiding starvation. On a slightly higher level, it might be to please your family or dinner guests. If the goal is to lose 14lb in weight, the motivation might be to feel better about yourself – or it might be something more specific, like preparing for your wedding day.

At its most basic, motivation is about the 'stick and the carrot' – fear and reward. This is something that great leaders innately understand. For example, the Roman Emperor Hadrian, who ruled Rome from AD 117 to 138, had several motivational tools available to him. Most were of the 'stick' variety: he could banish someone from Rome and its territories, remove someone's citizenship, make someone a slave, or throw people to the lions. After all, Roman Emperors had a long tradition of ruling with fear to live up to. Instead, he proved a comparatively enlightened Emperor. He decreed that mines should be equipped with bathhouses, for example. The result: happy miners – and miner's wives – more motivated miners, more productive miners.

The workplace is a good example of how our ideas about motivation have changed over time. At the beginning of the 20th century, the average worker was viewed as inherently lazy, someone that would only work as quickly as they were made to. The multi-talented American Frederick Taylor – inventor, tennis champion and perhaps the world's first management consultant – developed the concept of scientific management. His big idea was to time everything so that everyone knew how long a task should take. Then it was just a matter of timing the workers to make sure they are working at optimum speed.

Understandably, treating people like machines didn't go down that well, and it wasn't long before the workers protested. The result was a shift in emphasis.

Douglas McGregor was a psychology professor at the Massachusetts Institute of Technology. His work, published in the 1960s, addressed the fundamental question of whether employees are self-motivating individuals or fundamentally lazy and as such, need continual monitoring. He called these two viewpoints Theory Y and Theory X. McGregor believed organizational conditions at work should be arranged 'so that people can achieve their own goals *best* by directing *their own* efforts towards organizational objectives'.

Another psychologist, Frederick Herzberg, looked at motivation in relation to job satisfaction. He defined motivation in terms of what he called hygiene factors and motivation factors: those serving people's animal needs and those meeting uniquely human needs.

Hygiene factors included administrative practices, benefits, company policies, interpersonal relations, job security, physical working conditions, salary and supervision. But these factors are not enough on their own to provide the 'motivation to work'; according to Herzberg, true motivation comes from other factors such as achievement, job satisfaction, personal development and recognition. The aim should be to motivate people through the job itself rather than through rewards or pressure.

In the workplace, the debate about motivation has been about how to motivate the workforce. But often you will see job adverts that list 'self-starter' or 'self-motivated' as a requirement. Motivation may be internal or external. You may be responsible for motivating others – your family, your work team. Others may be responsible for motivating you – your boss at work. But possibly the toughest kind of motivation, and the one I want to concentrate on, is where you have to motivate yourself.

Why is it tough? Because although there will often be other people to motivate you, you can't rely on it. There will always be situations where it is just you and the task at hand; you and your long-term goals. This is the toughest test. And it is part of personal responsibility. If you can motivate yourself, then any other motivating factors are a bonus.

It is also important to understand how to motivate yourself, what pushes your buttons, so that you can deal with those situations when you need to motivate others. There will always be a time when you need motivational skills. Even if it is only persuading the children to go to school willingly, getting your partner to do something other than lounge around on a Sunday morning or firing up your team to deliver its work project on time.

THE SCIENCE OF APPLIANCE

Scientists, or more precisely motivational theorists, have been studying what makes us do things for many years. Although there are still no definitive answers, there are many theories. Here are a few of the more important ideas.

Motivational theorists define motivation in various ways, the consensus being that it is an internal state – a need or desire – that activates or energizes behaviour towards some purpose.

Motivation is usually described as extrinsic (external to the person motivated) or intrinsic (an internal process). This basic division can be broken down even further. Theories about intrinsic motivation can be sub-divided depending on the source of the need: physical, mental or spiritual.

According to the scientists, mental needs can be connected to one of three things: cognition, affect, or conation.

Cognition is to do with the process of coming to know or understand something. So if you want to solve a problem, or find out why something happened, you are motivated by a cognitive factor.

'Affect' is how we emotionally connect with information and knowledge and our perceptions. So if we choose to behave in a way that makes us feel better or improves our feelings of self-esteem, we are motivated by affective factors. For example, once I knew what the buzz of winning a gold medal felt like, one motivating factor was to recapture that feeling. The emotions I felt during major competitions are fundamental reasons why I loved to compete and win.

One of my proudest moments came not when I won a gold medal, but when I got silver in the 100m backstroke in Barcelona. Standing on the podium. I looked into the crowd and saw my mum and dad. They had the broadest smiles on their faces and the surge of joy that gave me will stay with me forever.

Conversely, when I have been unsuccessful, I have had a real sensation of letting my friends and family down. I try to avoid that at all costs.

Finally, there is perhaps the most interesting aspect mental motivation – conation.

Conation is where the knowing and the emotions connect to behaviour. It is about why we do things. It is the proactive goal-oriented aspect of motivation. It is associated with the idea of freewill or freedom of choice. What are my goals? What am I going to do? Why am I doing this?

More than one reason

That winter's morning, like every other morning, once I'd dragged myself out of bed, my early morning route to the pool took me through central and north London. Snaking through Soho, past bedraggled businessmen and transvestites in six-inch heels. Crossing Oxford Street, then Wigmore Street, Gloucester Place and onto the A41. St Johns Wood, Swiss Cottage, Finchley and Hendon pass by in a bleary-eyed blur. Finally I finish my 20-minute drive and arrive at the Barnet Copthall Pools at 5.10am.

On this occasion, as I drove along, I mulled over my lack of motivation that morning. The problem was focusing on a single reason; in my case, it was getting the gold medal. But that wasn't enough. Because on some days, the idea of the gold medal seemed like a fantasy compared with the harsh reality of everyday life. It wasn't a compelling enough reason; it was too easy to brush aside.

I realized I needed more than that to motivate me. Forget whether I responded better to the stick or the carrot – I needed more than one reason. Then I could run through each reason whenever I felt unenthusiastic about my swimming, and at least one of them would motivate me to keep going.

It is the same for everybody. Many people find simply going to work a challenge. Those that find it hardest to be motivated often have only one reason to go – their salary. Some days, even that isn't important enough and they won't go at all. In many ways my desire to win a gold medal was the equivalent of other people's salaries. Some days it motivated me, other days I needed more.

I know it sounds strange, but it worked. I felt under less pressure because I knew there were a whole lot of good reasons why I was putting myself through the training grind.

REASONS TO BE CHEERFUL

It is no use just choosing any old reason at random. That's not going to work. Your reasons have to be personal; they have to be the things that push your buttons. It took me a while to find the reasons that worked for me.

It is worth noting that reasons are not goals. Goals are the end destination, your reasons are the motivating factors that get you there.

General or specific?

The beauty of having multiple motivating factors is that they can be whatever you like – whatever is important to you. In fact, the more varied they are, the better. The aim is to have every eventuality covered.

A reason can be very detailed and specific: 'I need to give this presentation to company X tonight because I've earmarked the money to buy myself an electric drum set.' Alternatively, it can be more general: 'I need to give this presentation to company X tonight because I want to be more financially secure so that I can retire early.'

If the reason is too vague, though, it won't be any use.

Positive or negative?

Some people argue that it is unhealthy to be motivated by a negative thing – a negative remark or a fear. Admittedly, it would be nice if motivation by positive reasons was enough, but for many of us it is not. Fear – fear of failure, fear of losing your job, fear of your partner leaving you, fear of being disliked – is a powerful motivating factor.

Our cavemen ancestors went out to hunt because if they didn't, they would starve. If a wild animal attacked them, what do you think that they thought: 'I will run because I want to run, because I want to feel the physical exhilaration of running, the endorphins coursing through my body, because I will get fitter and healthier' or 'I will run because if I don't that animal will eat me!'?

Fear is a powerful motivator but it can be problematic.

FEAR AS A MOTIVATOR

The difficulty with fear as a motivating factor is that you tend to focus on the source of the fear rather than the task or goal. If the situation is 'I need to make a success of my business or I'm going to lose my house,' you can become so focused and consumed by the fear of losing your house that it can hinder you from achieving your goal.

A lot depends on what kind of person you are. Take the issue of job security, for example. I teach people how to improve their memory. Job security is fairly minimal these days, so transferable skills are increasingly important.

I could approach the issue with the people I teach from two angles. I could tell them that there is no chance that they will be working with the same company they are working with today in 30 years' time. Or I could say, 'Wouldn't it be great if you didn't have to work here? If you had the skills that gave you the choice about where to work? Skills that opened new doors?'

> One person might be terrified by the thought of being made redundant at some point in the future, but another might be driven to upgrade their skills. Ultimately, it depends on the kind of person you are.
>
> *David Thomas*
> *Grand Master of memory*

In our modern age, the problem with negative motivation is that it can lead to increased tension and stress. I find that I may be initially motivated in a negative way, perhaps by some comments that I felt were unfair, but then I begin to find positive motivators to help me work to the same goal. It is almost as if the negatives help me create the goal and then I work out why and how I am going to do it.

Connecting with goals

It is essential to take time to figure out what you want to achieve and what your definition of success is. As I mentioned in Chapter 3, without knowing your goals it is much more difficult to work out what your motivating factors are.

Similarly, if you are responsible for motivating others, you need to understand what their goals are. To jump straight in without determining the hopes, fears and desires of your team will mean limited buy-in and poor long-term outcomes. Often when a manager, coach or leader does this, they are trying to force their own goals, beliefs and motivators onto the individuals concerned. Success is far more likely if time is taken to get to know all the individuals concerned and help them determine what their motivating factors are.

Friends and family

Most goals, especially the tough ones, will impact on friends and family. There is the effect of the preparation and build-up as you work towards your goal, plus the effects following success or failure. The sacrifices you have to make may cause friction and problems in your relationship with friends and family.

This is often one of the most difficult aspects of motivation and goal pursuit. If you focus on the effects of your actions on your friends and family, it can be a powerful demotivator.

During my swimming career I would always train on either a Saturday or a Sunday, the only exception being when I was away competing. This meant I hardly ever attended family celebrations or visited friends. I made a point of not focusing on this. Instead I concentrated on how proud my family were when I represented my country, and especially so when I won gold. How my achievements improved my standard of living and theirs.

ORDINARY PEOPLE, EXTRAORDINARY LIVES

In 1909, Isaac Stringer, Bishop of Selkirk – the Yukon region of Canada – was heading cross-country with a fellow missionary and a guide. Stringer was hardened to this kind of travel, having lived with the Eskimos as a missionary for many years. Unfortunately, on this particular occasion, the guide became ill, so Stringer and his companion had to turn back and retrace their steps across the same mountains the guide had just led them through.

They were soon lost. Food was short, and living off the land close to impossible because of the severity of the winter. Soon they were living off grape-nuts and squirrels. When that ran out, the starving but resourceful Bishop turned to a more unorthodox food source. The two men built a fire. Then they took of their sealskin boots, boiled them for seven hours, baked them, and ate them. Stringers diary entry for Thursday 21 October 1909 reads: 'Breakfast off sealskin boot, soles and tops boiled and toasted. Soles better than uppers. Soup of small scraps of bacon and spoonful of flour (the scrapings of the flour bag), the last we had; tired; hands sore; took a long time to pack up.' Fortunately for Stringer and his companion, they stumbled into civilization along the Peel River shortly afterwards and were saved.

Team members

Much of our life is spent working with others in some sort of a team. Sometimes we may be lucky enough to pick the team ourselves: we are able to create the perfect blend of personalities and skills. However, more often then not, we find ourselves within a diverse group of individuals with varying skills and competencies.

From the role you have within the team and from your relationship with the other team members, you will find many reasons for working towards your goals. It may be the benefit the other team members will gain from achieving your goal, or the team's goal. It may be the sense of responsibility to the team – not to let them down or to prevent them from achieving the team objective.

Personal development

I like to be learning all of the time, whatever I turn my hand to. It might be something new in my training programme, a climbing technique, or understanding the intricacies of the various industries I work in.

All goals provide opportunities to learn. Even if it is something you have done before, you can be motivated by trying to do whatever it is that little bit better: play a musical instrument more proficiently, improve your cooking, master those presentational skills, or do that run just a little quicker. Continuous learning, constant development. If you approach life like this, then those difficult tasks become far more enjoyable.

Altruism

Charities survive and do their good work through the generosity of others, whether it is via the donation of money, goods and services, or time. Maybe you can find or include some charitable element to your goals that helps motivate you towards success.

Ethical or spiritual foundation

Motivating factors that directly align with your ethical and spiritual beliefs will be extremely powerful. There are many examples where individuals that have been fuelled by strong moral beliefs have achieved incredible things: people such as Mother Theresa, Mahatma Ghandi and Nelson Mandela have changed the course of history.

Whilst your goal may not be quite so grand, and not all of your motivating factors will have an integral element of your spiritual or ethical beliefs, it is imperative that they in no way contradict them.

Body image

With the influence of today's media, people are now more aware and critical of their own body image then ever before. Weight loss and weight gain, hairstyles and colour, muscle tone and posture. People are putting a higher priority on some of these things then ever before. It may be that in achieving your goal you are also having a positive impact on your own perceived body image.

Financial gain

You will perhaps think it strange that I have left the notion of financial gain as a motivator to the very end, after all most people will cite their salary as the main reason for them going to work. Of course most people need an income, otherwise they would stop working, but I feel that financial gain can become a negative issue all too quickly.

How often do you hear people talk about their salary in a positive way? It is far more likely that you have heard them say 'I deserve more', 'they don't pay me enough' or 'did you hear what bonus Jones in sales got, it just doesn't seem right?'

It is far healthier to focus on how the financial gain will impact upon your other motivating factors – your family, friends, your personal development, lifestyle and altruistic nature.

MASLOW, MOTIVATION AND PERSONALITY

In his book *Motivation and Personality*, published in 1954, Dr Abraham Maslow hypothesized that people are motivated by a hierarchy of needs. As each level of needs is met, individuals progress to higher-level motivators.

Maslow's hierarchy of needs is often represented as a pyramid. Each level of the pyramid is dependent on the previous level. For example, a person does not feel the second need until the demands of the first have been satisfied.

There are five basic layers of Maslow's hierarchy of needs:

1. Physiological needs. These needs are biological – the needs for oxygen, food, water and a relatively constant body temperature. These are the strongest because they are required for survival.
2. Safety needs. Except in times of emergency or social disintegration, adults do not experience their security needs. Children, however, often display signs of insecurity and their need to be safe.
3. Love, affection and belonging needs. People have needs to escape feelings of loneliness and alienation and give (and receive) love, affection and the sense of belonging.
4. Esteem needs. People need a stable, firmly based, high level of self-respect, and respect from others in order to feel satisfied, self-confident and valuable.
5. Self-actualization needs. According to Maslow, the need for self-actualization is 'the desire to become more and more what one is, to become everything

that one is capable of becoming.' Self-actualization is when the individual achieves their own personal potential. 'A musician must make music, an artist must paint, a poet must write, if he is to be ultimately at peace with himself. What a man can be, he must be,' said Maslow.

If these needs are not met, the person feels restless, on edge, tense, and lacking something.

Maslow believed that the only reason that people would not move through the needs to self-actualization is because of the hindrances placed in their way by society – including their employer. Work can be a hindrance, or can promote personal growth.

EMBRACE THE CHALLENGE

The more reasons you have to do something, the more likely it is that you will achieve your goal. Sure, if you have 105 reasons, it may take until number 95 that you feel like attacking your goal, but you still will. The reasons already outlined are just suggestions, some which have worked for me. You must find your own reasons to embrace your challenge, whatever that challenge is. Just make sure there is more than one.

FIVE

All or nothing

We must remember that one determined person can make a significant difference, and that a small group of determined people can change the course of history.
Sonia Johnson

We must all hang together or most assuredly we shall hang separately.
Benjamin Franklin

*Coming together is a beginning.
Keeping together is progress.
Working together is success.*
Henry Ford

SWIMMING IN DIFFERENT DIRECTIONS

In Atlanta, my main focus was the 400m freestyle, the 100m backstroke and the medley relay. But, once again, all my hard work was jeopardized when I picked up a viral chest infection a week before the competition. Still, I was the world record holder for the 400m freestyle, so I remained confident. If I could equal or, better still, break the world record again, the chances were that I would win.

On race day I felt good and swam hard. When I looked up at the clock, it read 4.31:87. I had equalled my world record. The only problem was that two other swimmers had broken it. It was a disappointing bronze medal for me.

Two days later, I won silver in the 100m backstroke. Although relatively pleased with my performance, it still wasn't the medal for which I had trained for four years. I wanted gold, not silver or bronze.

It was all down to the very last race of the competition – the medley relay. My last opportunity to win a gold medal.

SWIMMING BY NUMBERS

At the Paralympics, there are ten swimming categories for people with a physical disability. As someone with a very minimal disability, a single below the knee amputation, I compete in Class 10.

As the class number descends, the swimmer's disability is more comprehensive. Athletes in Classes 1 or 2 are likely to be people with high-level spinal injuries, multiple amputations or severe cerebral palsy. As a Class 10 swimmer, I would not normally compete against swimmers from other classes. It would be like boxers in different weight categories competing against each other.

The only time that categories are combined is in the relays. I competed in the 34-point relay, where teams pick the best combination of swimmers they can, as long as they don't exceed 34 points. For example, you could have one swimmer from Classes 7, 8, 9 and 10, or you may decide to use two each from Classes 7 and 10. There are many different combinations and this often leads to thrilling races, where the lead changes several times.

In Atlanta, I swam the last leg of the relay as a Class 10. The other team members were Classes 7, 8 and 9. The Germans were the main competitors for the gold medal, but I was convinced that we had a team that could beat them, as long as I was in touch with the German swimmer when I dived in on the last leg.

Going last in a relay is fantastic when the team is doing well, but demoralizing when you are some way behind. After the backstroke leg, we were level with Germany. Then came the breaststroke and Germany's Stefan Loeffler had an incredible swim. Suddenly we were 12 metres behind. My heart sank. It looked like silver or worse once again.

Giles Long made up some ground against the colossal German swimmer Detlef Schmidt, but by the time it was my turn to dive in, we were still seven metres down.

I put in a big effort and, with 50 metres to go, had somehow managed to get back within touch of the German. I could see him just in front of me in the next lane. As the pain kicked in with 25 metres to go, I was only one metre behind. In the final few metres I was almost level.

As the lactic acid thundered through my veins and slowed my already exhausted muscles, I struggled to maintain my technique to the end. I slammed my hand against the wall and spun around to look at the scoreboard. I had given every last scrap of energy.

I tried to read the scoreboard, but the evening sun was in my eyes. As I held my hand up to my eyes to shield them, the entire German team punched the air in unison. We had lost by 12 one-hundredths of a second. Spread 12 one-hundredths of a second over four years of gruelling training and it spreads very thinly.

To say I was disappointed is an understatement of some proportion. It was a bit like winning the lottery, but leaving the ticket in your trouser pocket when you put them in the washing machine. I was devastated. Sure, it was only a swimming race, but to me it was the culmination of four years of intense preparation and personal sacrifice. The gold medal was within touching distance … and then it was gone.

As with any other competition, I went through a process of evaluation, to see what could be learnt and improved upon. One thing was certain: we couldn't have trained much harder than we did. I couldn't find a reason for the team finishing second best. As the days passed, the race continued to haunt me. I had a repeated nightmare in which I would be swimming the final five metres of the race; every time I touched the wall I would wake up and disbelievingly look at my silver medal by the side of my bed.

It took two and a half months before I realized what had happened. Visiting my parents one weekend, my Mum asked if I wanted to keep any videos of the BBC coverage she recorded during the Games. I was still so upset about the outcome that

I didn't really want to go through them, but I decided to flick through a few quickly before they were erased. I watched the relay final the whole way through. Same story, same result. But then I noticed something during a short section towards the end. There we were, all four of us on the medal podium – two of us with beaming smiles on our faces; two of us looking devastated.

It was then I realized what was wrong. Training hard was fine, but it wasn't enough. We had to compete as a team. Not as four individuals. You might think that it's obvious. But it isn't. When you focus on a task so intently, with such commitment, it is easy to forget that regardless of how well you do as individual, you will always be second best if you don't perform as a team.

Buy-in

At the time I was 'leader by default'. I am sure that you know someone like this. They are in charge of a team because they are technically good at their job, and maybe they have been around the longest, but they don't necessarily have the leadership skills required. I certainly didn't. My leadership style was straight out of the *How to be a Roman Emperor* manual. It was a dictatorship rather than a democracy. I spoke but didn't listen. There wasn't a lot of empathy going either. I was task-oriented.

The result: failure to achieve buy-in from my team for my objectives. I'm not sure they even knew what my objectives were. On reflection, I didn't know what their objectives were either. So we had the crazy situation of a group of world-class individuals competing in Atlanta without any established team objective.

We may have looked like a team, but we weren't an efficient team. When the individuals in a team have different objectives, they are unlikely to reach their full potential. In our team, two of us wanted gold, and nothing less. And the other two were happy with any medal, regardless of the colour.

In fact, one team member was so concerned that he would get the team disqualified that he lost valuable time in the change-over. A year earlier at the European Championships he took a flyer – a faulty takeover – where he dived in a fraction of a second before the incoming swimmer had touched. We were disqualified and Germany went on to win.

As a team, we weren't that supportive. So this time he waited... and waited... and waited. He didn't dive in until he was absolutely certain the incoming swimmer had touched. It was only a matter of a few tenths of a second. But then we only lost by 12 hundredths of a second. Do I blame him? No. I blame myself. If I had spent more time focused on the team, and less on myself, we would have all been aware of his fears, been able to discuss them, and hopefully overcome them. And we would have all collectively decided on a team objective.

GETTING TEAMS TO WORK

When working in a group, you must be absolutely clear on what you are trying to achieve and what success looks like. I use the What (is the problem) How (are we going to tackle it) When (time frame) and Who (is going to do it).

There can be no compromise. Don't allow personalities to dominate. Focus on what you are trying to achieve and leave the meeting knowing what is going on and what has been decided.

Etienne de Villiers
Chairman of the ATP

WHO IS ON YOUR TEAM?

Legend has it that President John F. Kennedy was taking a tour of NASA, stopping occasionally to talk to the employees. 'What's your job at the facility?' the President asked one man. 'My job is to help put a man on the moon,' the man replied. He was a janitor.

It's a great illustration of the power and scope of teams. No person could put a man on the moon on their own, yet in a specialized team they managed it. And the janitor? He was as much of the team as the top scientists or the astronauts. If he had performed the tasks assigned to him badly he could have prevented one of the greatest achievements of the human race.

Teamwork and co-operation have a long history. The evidence from cave paintings suggests that hunters co-operated in the Stone Age. Together they could accomplish feats that they were unable to accomplish alone. For most of us, food is a little easier to come by these days, but teamwork is just as important.

Regardless of who you are, you are part of a team – unless you are a hermit living in the middle of nowhere, that is. You are probably part of a team at work, you maybe part of team called 'family', it may be just you and your partner, or you may play in a sports team. You may not realize you are part of a team. Equally, you may not realize who is on your team.

Swim team

You have probably realized by now that I am a very motivated person. Any team I've been a member of that has won gold has, inevitably, been highly motivated. But success is only a beginning, and once my swim team had won gold medals, we wanted to be even better and achieve greater things.

We continued to search for new talent and nurture it, but we also re-evaluated what the 'swim team' really meant. Who was in the team? The swimmers, obviously. But then there were all the other people involved: doctors, nurses, physiologists, sports psychologists, biomechanists, physiotherapists, team managers, coaches and even the people responsible for getting the pool ready for us to train in.

At times, the swimmers felt like the rest of the team weren't 100% committed to getting us onto the podium with the gold medal around our necks. Physiotherapists took holidays at times when the swimmers were most likely to need treatment. Biomechanists sometimes took too long to give feedback to the swimmers. The director of swimming focused his energies inappropriately. The pool staff didn't get the pool ready for training in time.

Individually, these problems were innocuous enough; together, however, they had an impact. Rather like the factory worker who doesn't pack a product properly. Once is not an issue; done repeatedly, it negates the hard work of the sales team.

Perhaps what we, the swimmers, didn't appreciate is that maybe these people didn't feel part of the team. Maybe they didn't understand how important they were to the process of winning. We had to make sure they appreciated their importance and that we appreciated them.

My coach at the time, Lars Humer, worked tirelessly at including everyone in the process of winning a gold medal. He never missed an opportunity to reinforce the message that everyone had an impact on the team's ability to succeed. It is not like a quick-fix pill that you can take once and forget about. It is more like cleaning your teeth – it needs to be done daily. It is a cultural change.

In Athens, my last Paralympic Games, the freestyle relay team swam faster that it had ever done before. It broke the world record previously held by China both in the heats and the final.

It was a terrific team performance. But for me, the highlight of that success was not the performance at Athens; it came when I returned. I was at the Manchester Aquatics centre with Lars to do a week of detraining (that is, winding down both physically and psychologically).

Phil Wood was a duty manager at the pool. He was responsible for making sure that our training facility was always ready for us to use. He came up to Lars and told him how much he had enjoyed watching the Athens Paralympics on television and how proud he was to see the team doing so well. Then he said something that made all that focus on teamwork worthwhile. 'I *am* part of that team, aren't I?' he said. And he was.

HOW TEAMS WORK

There has been plenty of research into teams and effective teamwork. Much of it has been to do with the way people work in organizations, because co-operation and teamwork in the workplace is critical to the success of organizations. In offices around the world, pictures of rowing crews and tug-of-war teams hang on office walls exhorting employees to be 'good team players'.

Lucky managers are dispatched to secluded corporate retreats, spa resorts and luxury hotels where they bond with colleagues. Less fortunate managers head for outward-bound camps where they trudge up mountains, abseil down cliff faces and build rafts with little more than empty oil drums, elastic bands and team spirit.

How do teams form? According to celebrated US academic Professor Bruce W. Tuckman, there are four phases of team development: forming, storming, norming and performing. In Tuckman's model of group development, teams have to go through a sequence of events before they are fully formed. Each stage has a task element and a relationship element.

In forming the team, members are finding out about the team's goals and any rules – providing comprehensive information helps with this. On the relationship side, team members test each other and jockey for position. Clearly defined roles help at this stage: this includes identifying a leader.

During the storming phase, the team goes through a period of revolution. Team members challenge both the tasks and the authority of the leader. It's essential to adopt the right approach at this stage: bury the disagreement and the team is storing up bitterness and resentment which will prove destructive later; exaggerate it, or allow it to continue for too long, and there is tension and hostility.

At norming time, the team is beginning to get it together. It's co-operating, communicating and sharing responsibility. It's beginning to feel and behave like an effective team.

Finally, we have performing. The team has become highly effective and acts together to solve problems. Team members have assumed suitable roles. They act interdependently.

Another famous piece of research into teamwork was conducted by Professor Meredith Belbin in the 1960s. Belbin studied teamwork at Henley Management College in the UK. Team members took a series of personality and psychometric tests. From his observations, Belbin discovered that certain combinations of personality-types performed more successfully than others. He identified nine archetypal roles required to make up an ideal team (see *Belbin's nine archetypal team members*, below).

BELBIN'S NINE ARCHETYPAL TEAM MEMBERS

Which one are you?

Completer: diligent, hardworking, meticulous; meets deadlines. Worries about not finishing tasks. Not good at delegation.

Co-ordinator: not always the brightest, but self-assured; a good administrator and organizer. Often chairs meetings.

Implementer: steady and efficient; makes things happen. Good at translating ideas into action. Very disciplined and well-organized. Can get stuck in routines and not that open to change.

Monitor evaluator: evaluates options and judges situations well. Good strategic overview. Not charismatic or inspiring. Steady.

Plant: unpredictable, unorthodox, left-field; a creative problem-solver. Poor social skills – at least with 'average' people. Low boredom threshold.

Resource investigator: great at the start of a task. Good communicator, motivates and enthuses. Outgoing. Soon loses interest and wants to move on to something new.

Shaper: go-getter; a fast-moving, dynamic, can-do person. Pushes, cajoles and forces teams to perform. Edgy, loses temper, shouts and storms out, but will get team through difficult challenges.

Specialist: not a great team player. An entrepreneurial self-starter with specialist skills or knowledge.

Teamworker: the glue that binds the team together; arbitrates, diffuses tension, sympathizes, listens, creates cohesion, socially perceptive and intuitive. Not a leader, a great decision-maker or one for quick action.

Belbin's team roles are still widely used, but more recent research on teams has considered other aspects of teamwork. Belbin viewed the team as an entity made up of individuals, where the success of the team depends on the individual elements carrying out their roles successfully. More recent studies have looked at teams as a whole rather than a group of individuals – looking at the collective competencies required to bring about effective performance.

One piece of research suggests that the degree of motivation a team has to complete a task, and how confident they are of completing it, are crucial collective competencies. This could explain the concept of team spirit. A team that has built up a repository of success and experience of overcoming adversity is likely to perform better than one that has no sense of collective identity or a poor track record.

To build an effective team:

- Don't speak for other team members – let them speak for themselves.
- Do make consensus decisions. If you can't, respect majority decisions.
- Don't bury conflict; deal with it.
- Do treat individual contributions as belonging to the group, not the individual.
- Don't ridicule contributions from other group members.
- Do communicate problems openly.
- Don't be disrespectful to other team members.
- Do co-operate.
- Don't compete.

LEAD, FOLLOW, EXECUTE

I have discussed at teams, how they are formed, and what kinds of roles team members play – but when it comes to leading, following and delivering within a team, how does it actually work?

- **Lead.** Traditionally teams have a single leader whose role it is to inspire, motivate and direct task completion. Research shows, however, that the role of the leader and the nature of leadership within groups need not be so conventional. Leadership occurs at all levels of an organization. In teams, different leaders may emerge depending on a given situation – so there is a blurring of roles between leaders and followers. Also, depending on the situation, a leader may have many different roles: creating the conditions for the team members to complete tasks by motivating, inspiring, mediating, directing – it could be any of these. Especially important is the role of leader in communicating a vision to those that have to deliver, and obtaining buy-in (see Fig. 5.1).
- **Follow.** Followers drive forward the initiatives set out by the team or team leaders. They plan and implement those plans. Some may be managers interfacing between leader and follower. The vision is communicated between followers. Good followers are essential for team effectiveness.
- **Execute.** Both leader and followers must perform their relative functions. If their relationship is underpinned by a culture of trust, communication and development, then there will be buy-in for the task and long term vision and, hopefully, execution.

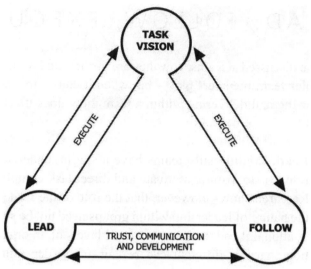

Fig. 5.1 Both the leader and follower base actions on a shared task and vision. *Trust, communication and development* is a two-way process.

FOLLOW THE LEADER

The subject of leadership deserves a book all of its own; indeed, there are many tens of thousands of books on the subject. It is worth mentioning in passing, because even if you are someone who does not perceive yourself as a leader, you may find yourself in leadership situations from time to time.

When it comes to leadership, there is what the leadership theorists – the people who study leadership for a living – think about leadership, and what I think – a person who has had to take a leadership role in a number of different situations.

A quick history of leadership theory

- **The Great Man theory** (Great Women were generally disregarded at the time). Leaders are born with innate talents that cannot be taught.
- **The trait theory.** Effective leaders have certain traits that can be learnt if we can identify what those traits are.
- **Transactional leadership.** The relationship between leader and followers is based on an exchange of value that is mutually beneficial: 'You do this task, then I reward you.' The reward might be psychological, political or economic in nature.
- **Transformational leadership.** The relationship between leader and followers is based on the leader helping the followers to aim for certain goals that meet the wants and needs, aspirations, and expectations of both leader and followers. It is about engaging with followers.
- **Charismatic leadership.** Leaders are charismatic, heroic types. They inspire and motivate, and lead partly through sheer force of personality.
- **Authentic leadership.** Leaders should not try and adopt leadership styles that are not part of their natural make-up, and be someone they are not. The followers will find them out. Instead, they should be true to their own values, beliefs etc.
- **Change leadership.** Effecting change requires a special sort of leader. It needs a leader that is prepared to grab an organization or team by the scruff of the neck and set it on a new course. It requires top-down decision-making, quick action, tough leadership

- **Distributed leadership.** Either leaders are distributed throughout the organization or team, or the role of the leader, the power of the leader, is assumed by different people at different times.

My own take on leadership is that bits of all of the above are probably true at different times. In my experience as a leader, there are times when participative leadership is required and times when a more dictatorial style is appropriate. Different people may assume leadership roles at different times and for different tasks; however, when things go wrong, the leader is usually the person who takes responsibility. They are the person everyone looks to for an explanation of what happened. (Note: they are not necessarily the person that gets the blame, though.)

There is even evidence that some teams can perform well with no designated leader at all. From 1994 to 2000, coach Ric Charlesworth guided the Australian women's hockey team – the Hockeyroos – to successive World Cup and Olympic gold medals. The team was unique, not just because of its achievements, but because it had no designated captain or vice-captain. The idea was that everyone would take responsibility for performing well and it wouldn't just fall on the shoulders of one person.

TEAMBUILDING

In the early stages of a team developing, I try to get the team to establish some ground rules. This is particularly useful with a team of inexperienced individuals. I recently recommended this to a group of graduates that were failing to work together as a team. The 'rules' simply act as a framework within which to operate. Such rules might include:

- If no leader has been appointed, then appoint one.
- A leader takes responsibility for achieving the aim.
- The team takes responsibility for contributing to the aim and assisting the leader in achieving the aim.
- No idea should be immediately discounted but discussed and assessed.
- Everyone should have an opportunity to contribute.
- Timescales are fixed and should be achieved.

I never expect a group of people to immediately gel. A team takes time to build.

Lesley Garside
Operations Director, Northgate HR

TEAM TALK

In my experience there are a number of important issues relating to teams. In fact, although these points relate to teams, most work on a personal, individual level and will also improve personal performance. Indeed, many are covered in more depth elsewhere in this book.

Define clear objectives

If we define objectives as something sought-after and aimed for, then it stands to reason that we should be clear about them. A team must define its objectives so that the entire team is agreed on what it wants to achieve, and also on how it is going to achieve it.

The clarity of the objectives is the key. For example, someone in the family may say: 'We need to be happier.' It sounds great, but it's meaningless if 'happier' is not adequately defined. A better goal is: 'We need to be happier by spending more time together.'

Now we have an objective that everyone can understand, but it could still do with some clarification: 'We need to manage our time better so that we can take a holiday together.' The result: a happier family. OK, I know what you are thinking – but a holiday works for some people.

The point is we now have an objective that is easier for everyone to work towards because it is more clearly defined. Objectives can be continually broken down and defined in more detail. Often it is easier to consider and complete goals bit by bit. Otherwise a goal can appear overwhelming or too daunting.

Identify team roles

Team roles should be as well-defined as possible. Team members must understand their responsibilities and what they are accountable for – thus you avoid the 'No-one told me to do that' situation when something doesn't get done and no-one knows who was responsible for doing it.

Get involved

It is one for team members to be committed to working towards the team goals; it is another for them to be involved and to believe in the team goals.

If you develop a simple mission statement with other members of the team it will help get buy-in from everyone.

People perform better if they believe in what they are doing and they have a common purpose, rather than just expending effort (physical or mental) without emotional engagement.

In our team we trust

There has to be openness, honesty and trust within a team or it won't perform. Team members must be treated equally. Don't just focus on the strong members of the team – it may be a natural thing to do, but it can be divisive. Remember to include the weaker team members as well. If you improve their performance, you improve the team's performance.

Setting standards

A team needs goals, but it also needs a measure of how it is performing with respect to those goals. It is possible to set standards anywhere on a scale of low to high. However, if you set them low, don't expect people to exceed them willingly. Better to set them high and start as you mean to go on. The higher the standards you set, the better you will be.

Communication

A team can only succeed when team members at every level clearly understand where they are going, commit their support, and do what is required to achieve their goals.

If this is going to happen, everyone must take responsibility to proactively communicate. Team members must positively reinforce the team's objectives, clarifying the vision, discussing and resolving issues as and when they arise.

This is what I mean by a culture of communication – and the larger the team, the greater the need to actively share information, ideas and other intellectual resources.

WHO IS ON YOUR TEAM?

If you want to be an effective team member, you need to know who the team members are.

- Which teams are you a part of?
- Do you know who is on your team in each of those teams?
- Do you know what roles they play?
- Do you know who the weak and strong members of the team are?
- Who is the team leader?

GOING IT ALONE

No matter how independent or self-reliant you are, don't fool yourself that you can get by without being part of a team. You may be a fringe member, you may be a maverick figure within a group – either way, you still need to understand the basics about how teams work. The sooner you work out your role within the various teams you play a part in, the easier it will be to improve your performance. And with the right team around you, it is amazing what you can achieve.

SIX

Communication breakdown

*The single biggest problem in communication
is the illusion that it has taken place.*
George Bernard Shaw

*The finest language is mostly made up of
simple, unimposing words.*
George Eliot

TEAM TALK

Compared with the tension of a Paralympic Games, the European Championships are a far more relaxed affair for most of the competitors. Going into the 1999 championships in Braunschweig, Germany, the British swimming squad was expecting to get a good haul of medals.

For me, aside from my individual races, it was a chance to build the foundations of a British 4×100m freestyle relay team that could go on to win a medal at the Sydney Paralympics. I was one of the senior members and I knew that to be competitive at Sydney 2000, we would have to create a team with a single vision.

In Atlanta we were a team, but not a very efficient one. In Braunschweig, I was determined to make sure that I knew what the other team members wanted to achieve on the day of competition – not what I thought or imagined they wanted, but to actually hear from them in person. If we could identify one clear group objective, it would probably make the difference between silver and gold.

One issue was which leg of the relay each of us should swim. Usually we put the fastest swimmer last, the second-fastest first, and the remaining two swimmers in the middle spots. The problem is that while this sets the team up well in the race, it doesn't always play to the strengths of the swimmers. In Braunschweig, I wanted a team order that suited each swimmer and made the whole team stronger.

Matt Walker was one of the newest members of the team. Matt had joined the Great Britain team the year before for the World Championships in Christchurch. He has mild cerebral palsy. One symptom is a slight tremor that affects his control in certain aspects of his swimming. Braunschweig was his first opportunity to swim in the relay team and he was looking forward it.

This time, unlike Atlanta, I wanted to make sure that we communicated as a team, and that we all agreed on the team objectives. So when we first arrived in Germany, I asked Matt which relay leg he wanted to swim.

'I suppose you want me to swim in the middle some-where,' he said, aware that his best time was the slowest of the team.

'Matt I want you to be happy. The happier you are, the faster I think you'll swim.'

'Well I'm not very confident with my takeovers.'

Matt's tremors mean that he can be a bit unsteady on the starting block. It's not a problem in his individual race when he has more time to sort it out; the relay, however, is a whole different swimming race. There's more pressure. In a swimming relay changeover, your feet must be touching the starting block when the incoming swimmer touches the pool wall. But to get a fast changeover, the next swimmer will start to dive in, just as their team-mate is about to finish. A rolling start like this can save the team half a second. But it is a very fine call and much more difficult if you are unstable on the block. Consequently, Matt got a lot more nervous – and so did the rest of the team.

'Would you like to go first, then?' I asked him.

'Yeah, that would be great!'

'OK. It's a deal. If you want to go first, you can. I'm sure you will swim faster in that position – and if you swim faster, the team is more likely to win.'

Matt seemed a little surprised both at the sudden outbreak of team communication and that he was getting a choice. I could tell by the look of relief, though, that we were doing the right thing.

As for the rest of the positions in the relay, we simply worked around the change. Jody Cundy, a great starter and the second-fastest swimmer in the team, normally started the relay. But once he knew how Matt felt, he realized it was better for everyone if Matt went first. So Jody and David Roberts and I simply took up the remaining positions.

So how did it all work out? As we walked out for the relay final, all the team members had already won individual medals. A gold medal would be the perfect way to end the Championships. On the first leg, Matt did a great job. Although I didn't know it until later, he swam a personal best. By the time I hit the water, we were already in the lead.

Even if I had gone steady we would probably have won. But I didn't just want to win; I wanted to win in style. I wanted to see exactly what we were capable of. I worked as hard as I could for the full 100m. When I touched the timing pad and looked up at the scoreboard, I had the satisfaction of knowing that not only had we won gold, but we had broken the world record by three seconds.

FRITZ

One communication technique I use is the Fritz technique. One of America's most successful college football coaches gathered his new players together during the first game of the season. He then turned to his big defensive tackle, a guy named Fritz, and asked him 'What are the plays?', and Fritz would call the plays. This continued for the whole of the first half when finally, the quarterback could take it no longer and asked his coach why he insisted on asking Fritz what the plays were all the time.

The coach replied: 'Fritz is the dumbest guy in the whole team and I know that if he understands what plays to call then you're all going to know what to do'.

I always wanted to ensure that everyone knew what was going on and would encourage people to raise their hands in meetings and say 'I'm Fritz' when in doubt about a particular point or subject.

Etienne de Villiers
Chairman of the ATP

GETTING THE MESSAGE ACROSS

Communication is an essential part of life; society and civilization depend upon it. Without a sophisticated means of communication, humans would probably still be living in caves. Language dates back to the beginning of civilization and beyond: at least three thousand years before the birth of Christ, the Sumerian people were speaking and writing in their own language. What were they talking about? The usual things, apparently. In his book *The Third Stage in the Creation of Human Language*, Alexander Jóhannesson wrote: 'The first human needs are food and drink and the appeasement of sex; primitive speech must be closely related to these needs.'[1] He doesn't mention the weather.

Communication breakdown has an equally impressive history. The Sumerians may have been a progressive people in ancient world terms, but when it came to gender equality, they

---

[1] Alexander Jóhannesson, *The Third Stage in the Creation of Human Language*, Leitfur and Blackwell, 1963.

Table 6.1 My relay team mates, 1996–2004

Atlanta 1996 medley relay	Shaun Uren	Backstroke specialist
	Iain Matthews	Gold medallist in the 100m breast stroke at the 1992 Barcelona Paralympics
	Giles Long	Gold medallist in the 100m butterfly at the Atlanta and Sydney Paralympics Bronze medallist in the same event in Athens
Braunschweig 1999 freestyle relay	Matt Walker	Sydney and Athens Paralympian 6 Paralympic medals
	David Roberts	Sydney and Athens Paralympian 7 Paralympic gold medals
	Jody Cundy	Butterfly specialist 100m butterfly gold medallist Atlanta and Sydney Paralympics Bronze medallist in Athens
Sydney 2000 freestyle relay	Matt Walker	Sydney and Athens Paralympian 6 Paralympic medals
	David Roberts	Sydney and Athens Paralympian 7 Paralympic gold medals
	Jody Cundy	Butterfly specialist 100m butterfly gold medallist Atlanta and Sydney Paralympics Bronze medallist in Athens
Athens 2004 freestyle relay	Matt Walker	Sydney and Athens Paralympian 6 Paralympic medals
	Graham Edmonds	Sprint specialist and gold medallist in Athens
	David Roberts	Sydney and Athens Paralympian 7 Paralympic gold medals
	Robert Welborn	Made his debut at the Athens Paralympics, winning a gold and a silver medal

were in the Dark Ages. Women were chattels. If your husband died, you became the property of your husband's father or brother. You will often hear it said, usually after a misunderstanding, that women and men don't speak the same language; in ancient Sumer, they really *did* speak a different language. There were two dialects – the men's and the women's. Imagine the potential for miscommunication.

Today, there are around 6,900 known living languages.[2] That is plenty of potential for communication problems. But you don't need to be trying to talk to someone who speaks a different language to run into problems; communicating with people who speak the same language can be just as difficult.

Body talk

Communication isn't just about speaking or writing. Professor Albert Mehrabian, based at UCLA in the US, is a pioneer in the field of non-verbal communication – or body language. In one study concerning the communication of feelings and attitudes, he found that 55% of meaning from an exchange was connected to what a person could see, 38% to the tone, volume and speed of the sound, and just 7% to the actual words.

Non-verbal communication is largely unconscious. We may smile knowingly, or frown, yet in every person-to-person exchange, we give out countless nonverbal signals or cues. For example, unconscious facial expressions include the lip-pout, which signals disagreement or, in dating, harmlessness and availability; tense-mouth, a sign of anger, determination, or thoughtfulness; and the tongue show, a universal sign of

---

[2] Raymond G. Gordon (editor), *Ethnologue: Languages of the World* (15th edition), SIL International, 2005.

unspoken disagreement, disbelief, antipathy, displeasure or uncertainty.

When it comes to reading non-verbal cues, women have the edge. Several studies indicate that women are able to interpret non-verbal cues better than men. They are also more able to communicate the importance of relationships using non-verbal cues. Women make eye contact more often than men. They also smile more often.

For both sexes, building an understanding of non-verbal cues is time well spent. It can even save a relationship. As Burgoon *et al.* note in *Nonverbal Communication: The Unspoken Dialogue*: 'The absence of a hug at bedtime may be more telling to a spouse about the intimacy of the marriage than any other present cue.'[3]

MY SECRETS OF GOOD COMMUNICATION

From my experience in swimming, my public speaking career and my work in connection with the Teenage Cancer Trust, I have discovered that certain things affect my ability to communicate effectively.

Here then are a few 'secrets' of good communication. (I have focused on the spoken rather than the written word, as this is where most of my experience lies.) I am not suggesting that these tips will work for everyone or that everyone should slavishly follow them. All I can say is that they have worked for me, and hopefully they will work for you.

---

[3] J.K. Burgoon, D.B. Buller and W.G. Woodall, *Nonverbal Communication: The Unspoken Dialogue*, Harper & Row, 1994.

- listening;
- barriers to communication;
  - reputation;
  - prejudice;
  - keeping secrets;
- tailored communication;
- sound of silence;
- ebb and flow;
- body language and eye contact; and
- plain speaking.

Listening

Perhaps one of the most important things you can do if you want to improve your communication skills is to learn to listen properly. Communication is a two-way process. Lots of people are good at talking, but not so many are good at listening. Great communicators excel at both. As the Greek philosopher Epictetus said: 'We have two ears and one mouth so that we can listen twice as much as we speak.'

Poor listening skills can lead to misunderstanding and damage relationships. A simple example is a conversation where you can tell that the person you are talking to is thinking about what they are going to say next, rather than listening to what you are saying. We've all experienced it – it's annoying. It sends out the message that what you are saying is not important.

There are several things you can do to improve your listening skills. To begin with, make sure the non-verbal aspects are OK: face the person who is speaking, get close enough to hear what is being said, and watch for non-verbal cues. Try to gauge the emotional content of their communication.

Secondly, make sure that you have good listening manners. Don't butt in, especially not to correct the person speaking. Concentrate on what they are saying and not on what you are planning to say. Try not to always want the last word. Try not to be judgemental.

Finally, engage your brain before responding. Think about what you want to say before speaking. Be aware of any prejudices you may have and how they are likely to colour your response.

Breaking down the barriers

There are so many things that can prove a barrier to communication. It's not always possible to remove all the barriers, but at least if you can recognize some of them, you can try.

Reputation

Credibility is an important issue. In my experience from my speaking career, there are two types of people that you will encounter in life: those that require you to prove yourself in some way before they will listen to you, and those who will listen until they have a reason not to.

It is like the 'Is the glass half-empty or half-full?' syndrome: some people are optimists by nature whereas others are pessimists. Equally, some people are naturally cynical, some less so. When I give a talk, some people need to see the gold medal before they are willing to listen, some need to see the video, some even need to see my leg – they can't believe I walk as well as I do and need to see the proof.

Credibility is not automatic. It doesn't come with a title, degree or seniority. It is about knowledge and the ability to use it in a way that achieves a desired result. It is about action. It is about behaviour. It is about reputation.

Shakespeare, a man who understood the human condition better than most, understood the importance of reputation. It was a theme that ran throughout his plays. 'The purest treasure mortal times afford is spotless reputation,' said Mowbray in *Richard II*. Shakespeare reportedly observed of himself: 'I am my reputation.' You are, too.

A reputation isn't just for great men or women. It is not the sole province of presidents and prime ministers, of lawyers or doctors. We all have a reputation, good or bad. Just ask a few people who know you and you'll soon find out what yours is. You may be surprised. The word 'reputation' – meaning that which is generally believed about your character – is derived from the Latin *reputatio*, or reckoning. It is just as important today as it was in the 16th century. Your reputation is built upon values as well as abilities. Society attributes certain values to a good reputation, such as reliability, honesty, and integrity.

Whatever your values are, you must make a determined effort to live up them – this means consistency. If you build your reputation on honesty and reliability, you must not let those values slip. Tell one lie or let one person down, and it may undo years of good work. But if you build a good reputation – if you are constant and true to yourself – then credibility will be one barrier to communication that you should have no problem with.

Prejudice

There are countless examples of communication failure due to prejudice over colour of skin, sex, socio-economic group and age.

Have you ever stepped back and watched the majority of English people communicate when they are abroad? When faced with someone who doesn't speak English, what do they do? They assume the other person is stupid and perhaps a little deaf and start shouting, rather then trying to find an alternative way to communicate. Obviously communication is made more difficult when a common language is not shared, but deep down we all know that shouting will not help people understand.

Keeping secrets

Do you see yourself as an open person? Or are you guarded? Is your approach to life a collegiate, sharing one? Or is it more private and secretive? Most of us live in a free market economy, an economic system where competition determines who succeeds. At work we find ourselves in competitive situations with people from other companies, and internally with other colleagues. Naturally, in such situations we behave in a way that is to our own advantage. Of course while we may benefit, others, including our employers, may not.

Knowledge sharing is a good example. It is tempting to hoard knowledge in the hope that either you can use it to your advantage or that you can prevent others from benefiting from it. After all, 'knowledge is power', supposedly. Yet communication invariably involves an exchange of information. An unwillingness to share information can lead to poor communication, which in turn can lead to some very undesirable results.

Why don't people share knowledge? There are several reasons. Communication and the exchange of information require trust. I need to be able to trust someone with information I give them. Trust them not to steal it or pass it off as their own.

Equally, I may not realize the importance of the information I possess to another person. I may have a meeting tomorrow evening, but my partner has booked a restaurant table. It may not occur to me that coming home a couple of hours later than usual will cause problems. But I'll soon find out how important that information was to my partner.

Tailored communication

Tell two people the same thing and they will interpret the information differently. They may read the non-verbal signals differently. They may understand the content differently. If they pass that information on, it will become more distorted.

To avoid misunderstanding and to maximize the effectiveness of communication, it is important to tailor the communication for the audience.

I was once asked to speak in New York to a national sales force of approximately 300 people. When I was first booked, I was given a brief to deliver a motivational speech focusing on teamwork and the important role that a support team plays. The conference organizers were hoping to strengthen the relationships between the sales team and the back office staff. So I spent quite a while constructing a presentation to both inspire and strengthen the team.

When I arrived in New York three months later, I was told there had been some 'restructuring' within the business. They were moving the customer service centre to another country and planning to reduce the number of employees. In fact, it was likely that half of the people who were about to listen to my motivational teamwork speech the following morning would be losing their jobs within six months! No wonder the meeting planner that had booked me looked a little nervous. There was no way I could deliver the speech I had planned. That night proved to be a long one as I rewrote what I was going to say.

The next day, as I entered the auditorium, I could sense the downbeat feeling amongst the delegates, but I delivered a speech that was tailored to their situation. Instead of teamwork I focused on coping and embracing change. By the end of it the crowd were on their feet, and there was a general buzz around the place for the rest of the day. The client was both relieved and delighted.

Ebb and flow

One of the most famous speeches of all time was delivered by Martin Luther King on the steps at the Lincoln Memorial in Washington DC on 28 August 1963. Today, over 40 years later, millions of people can still tell you what the speech was about and even recite a couple of lines from it.

What gave this speech such an impact? One reason the speech is so good is that although King spoke for 16 minutes and 10 seconds, there was an ebb and flow, a rhythm to the speech, that carried people along. He didn't slam people with his best line, and then try and hold them there – instead, he took them on a journey that peaked with the two famous passages included here. The first approximately three-quarters of the way through:

> One day, right there in Alabama, little black boys and black girls will be able to join hands with little white boys and white girls as sisters and brothers. I have a *dream* today!

And the second as a resounding closing statement:

> Free at last! Free at last! Thank *God* Almighty, we are free at last!

For any communication longer than 15 minutes, there has to be some sort of ebb and flow. If you are preparing a presentation, do not try and get emotions to peak within the first few minutes and then hold them there. No audience can cope with that. No matter how good your final point is, a percentage of the audience will have drifted off. It is far better to bring them up and down several times and end with a powerful point.

The windows to the soul

In many cultures, the eyes are referred to as the 'windows to the soul'. The eyes can betray someone's nervousness or show steely intent. As we communicate information, the impact and interpretation of our words can vary greatly as we blink, gaze, flutter our eyelids, look at the floor or look straight back at someone. It is one of the most basic ways of expressing and detecting key emotions, such as trust, power, surprise or disappointment.

When I am delivering a speech, I will try and obtain some level of eye contact with as many people as I can. When I speak to a small group of say 50 people, I can be reasonably confident of making eye contact with all of the audience during a 45-minute presentation, thus creating a great sense of warmth and engagement.

Body language and gestures

Regardless of what an individual is saying, what do you think of people if they fail to gesture while speaking? Are they boring, stiff and unanimated? What do you think of someone who sits and talks to you with his or her arms folded?

A lively and animated communication style can capture the attention much more readily. If, when sitting at a meeting or discussion, you are leaning slightly forward, it communicates that you are approachable, receptive and friendly. Also, when it is your turn to listen, a nod of the head can offer a positive reinforcement and indicate that you are listening.

In addition to body language, you must also consider your proximity to those whom you are conversing with. We all have a boundary around us and we feel uncomfortable if it is crossed. This personal space varies from person to person and depends on the social situation, the other people present and the environment you are in. Signs such as totally avoiding eye contact and constantly backing away from you might indicate that you are too near and, as such, your communication is less effective.

Plain speaking

Everybody knows some jargon but the key is to only use it at appropriate times. I could describe a swimming race to some fellow swimmers like this –

'His transition phase was excellent and he was quickly into his stroke, breathing bilaterally. He had been working on his backend speed in training so it was no surprise that he negative split and PB'd in a 55 flat.'

– but the majority of people wouldn't understand it. So instead, I will say:

'He surfaced from his dive smoothly and was quickly into his swimming, breathing every three strokes. In training, he had been working on maintaining his speed at the end of his race, so it was no surprise that he did a personal best time of 55 seconds, swimming the second half of the race quicker then the first.'

When communicating, there has to be a balance between engaging the audience and ensuring that the picture is not cluttered with jargon and acronyms. Plain speaking is about delivering your communication in a way that matches the audience's ability to understand you.

Silence is golden

This chapter has been about communication – how to do it well and how not to do it. There are times, however, when saying nothing is better than saying something. Times when the sound of silence is the best communication tool of all.

It may sound strange, but silence can be an extremely powerful communication tool. A pause in the dialogue, for example, can show how committed you are to the statement that precedes it.

Alternatively, you may choose to stop talking until you have the full attention of the people you are communicating with. I had a teacher at school that was a master at this, standing silently at the front of the class until all eyes were focused on her.

Silence can also be a very useful tool when negotiating. Many people feel uncomfortable with silence. Rather than allow the silence, they will make concessions to fill what they consider an awkward pause in the conversation. Next time you are quoted a price for goods or services over the phone, try keeping quiet for a moment – you might get a pleasant surprise.

ORDINARY PEOPLE, EXTRAORDINARY LIVES

Fran Capo is not one to turn down a challenge. And that's an attitude that has got her a long way in life – and into some strange situations.

She started out as a stand-up comedienne and gravitated into a moderately successful media career – weather and traffic on radio. Until, that is, she was interviewed for a news article and asked what she planned to do next. At a loss for what to say, for some reason Capo blurted out: 'I'm thinking about breaking the *Guinness Book of World Records* for the fastest talking female.'

The article came out the next day and by that evening Capo was on the *Larry King Live* show attempting to break the record! Astonishingly, she succeeded – 545 words from the 91st Psalm in one minute. Her career took off.

Since then Capo has run a marathon, flown combat aircraft, rode a bike non stop for 100 miles, driven a racing car, gone diving with sharks, conducted a memorial service for the Titanic under the ocean at the wreckage site, and held a book signing on top of Mount Kilimanjaro.

FEEDBACK

It would be an out-and-out lie if I said that I agreed with all the feedback I have received, or to pretend that I have always enjoyed the process.

Occasionally I was asked to do something in training that I felt was outside of my capabilities. For example, when my coach told me that part of the day's training is set aside for hypoxic breathing, I would wince inside. Hypoxic breathing training involves increasing the number of arm strokes between each breath by one, until eventually I run out of air, then I decrease them back down again. It's a bit like doing shuttle runs, or driving the length of the country on holiday with three children in the back of the car. You know there's something good at the end – hopefully – it's just painful getting there.

What kind of feedback did I usually get when I did my hypoxic training? The in-your-face harsh kind. 'My Granny could do better than that and she's been dead six years,' was one notable favourite. But there is no point in trying to argue, especially if you have a good coach that you trust. In some ways, the situation made me handle the feedback process better: I was usually too tired and out of breath to argue, so instead I was forced to listen before jumping to conclusions or trying to justify my actions.

I know that my coach understood that I was doing my best, just as I know that he set challenges to help me be the best I could be, even if I find those challenges very difficult.

Feedback is absolutely essential as an athlete. We have to learn how to take it. No one enjoys being told they are doing something wrong, and for people who find it hard to take criticism, or accept orders, it is even more difficult. But you have to get used to it otherwise you never improve.

Outside of sport, however, there is a different culture. Feedback is just as essential in general day-to-day life, in the workplace or at home. The problem is that most of us are not trained to give feedback and not that used to receiving it. While some companies have a performance culture that encourages positive feedback and teaches people how to deal with it, most do not. In most cases, people do not know how to give or receive feedback.

I once attended a training course for people that wanted to improve their public speaking skills. Each participant chose a topic and then made a five-minute presentation on it. Following the presentation, they received feedback from the other delegates. What ensued was an uncomfortable session where the delegates were reluctant to give feedback and the presenter unwilling to receive it. Most delegates, in an attempt not to offend, gave bland, vaguely positive feedback that failed to provide any real indication of the presenter's abilities or where they could improve. On the rare occasion that someone tried to give constructive criticism, the presenter would instantly justify their actions. As a result, each person left the course believing that their presentation skills were excellent, only to suffer later when faced with the harsh realities of speaking in public.

FEEDBACK: TAKING IT AND DISHING IT OUT

Giving feedback

Do you plan your feedback? If you are leafing through notes and trying to figure out what you are going to say whilst the person is already in front of you, it will devalue the feedback. Give the impression that you have given careful consideration to what you are about to say and not that it is something you are making up on a whim. Even when time is short, I will always run a feedback conversation through in my head before I deliver it.

Is the feedback constructive? There is no point making negative comments that make no positive contribution about how someone can improve. The aim is to motivate an individual to change, not to demoralize them so they give up. If there is a negative element to what you have to say, make sure that you offer solutions too. For example to say 'Your demeanour was appalling when you made that presentation' is not as helpful as saying 'If you stand purposefully and make more eye contact when you present, you will find it easier to engage your audience.'

Is it personal? Feedback must be specific to the person but not an assassination of a personal characteristic. If you need to address personal issues, always do it one-to-one, and try to use analogies. Don't tell someone that they have a crap hairstyle, for example – instead, point out what difference appearances can make in different situations. Give examples. Only if this fails is it time to be blunt.

Are there too many points? People are not able to process excessive amounts of information. A basic guide is that between five and nine points are enough. Focus on a few main points.

When I teach swimming I will focus on one thing at a time, spending several minutes reinforcing a point and letting the pupil try the new skill before moving onto something else. Within an entire swimming lesson I will never work on more than five things and sometimes only one or two. I tend to think it is better to get an improvement in just one area than no change in several.

Am I being aggressive? Most people do not react well to aggressive people. They stop listening to them and start to think about how to retaliate or justify their actions. Deliver your feedback in a clear and calm manner. When I have been searching for a coach, I can normally tell within a few minutes if they will be able to do this. If their main way of communicating is to shout, then they are not right for me.

Do I take responsibility for my communication? Don't assume that someone has understood a piece of communication. Check. Does the behaviour of the individual reflect what you have tried to communicate? If not, it is not their fault – it is simply that the communication did not work. It is too easy to say 'Well, I told them and they are still not doing it!' – what this means is that although they may have heard the communication, you have not got them to buy into it. There can be many reasons for this; you need to find out which it is. Perhaps they don't consider what you communicated to be a priority – although they agree, they think it can wait. Or maybe they just plain disagree. With some of my team-mates I have sometimes had to recommunicate feedback in several different ways before a change in behaviour can be seen.

Receiving feedback

Don't interrupt. By interrupting, you may miss the one thing that will help you understand and improve what you are doing. When you interrupt, you may alter the planned feedback and just receive a knee-jerk reaction. I was once being given feedback following some work that I had delivered. I interrupted and instantly knew that I had broken the flow of my client. I left the meeting feeling that I had missed out on something.

Listen. As I have said already, listen and only listen to all that has been said. What I mean by that is, do not try and listen, and at the same time plan a response, and justify your actions. Try and understand why they are giving you this feedback and how they perceive your actions. When I listen to feedback from my coaches, I try to see things not only from my perspective but also from theirs. After all, they are just as keen for me to improve.

Clarify. Clarification is a key point in the feedback process. Even if you feel that you understand the feedback you have received, clarify it and listen to any reinforcements offered. It is very easy to misinterpret comments and act upon them inappropriately. My coach was usually very good at giving clear and specific feedback, but if he were to mention something about my stroke that could be improved on – having watched a race – I might then ask if it was consistent throughout the race or whether it was worse towards the end. The feedback then becomes more valuable. **Clarify.** Do it again.

Encourage feedback

I have developed a thirst for feedback. Without receiving it from my swimming coaches over the years, I would have never achieved my potential. I now spend my time trying to encourage my clients to do the same and it is a far more difficult proposition. Many businesses do not have a feedback culture – to them, feedback is as welcome as the sound of distortion you get when putting a microphone close to an amplifier.

I always ask people that attend my presentations what they enjoyed the most and which parts they felt were the most useful. I also make a point of asking which bits they didn't find useful.

- Ask open questions wherever possible. Closed questions will receive closed responses. Whenever possible, encourage people to provide you with detail about how your performance and actions can be improved.
- Determine what works well so that you can repeat it where appropriate. Asking people about areas where they thought you performed well helps to reinforce the positives. Sometimes you may think that something hasn't worked but your client, colleague or boss may disagree. They might be right.

- Ask what improvements can be made in a performance or action. Encourage people to find fault in what you do. Understand that they may deliver their feedback in an insensitive way, but still follow the rules for receiving feedback.
- Take it or leave it.

Once you have listened to everything and clarified it, decide whether you are going to act on it. This decision may be based upon a range of factors, including the actual advice itself as well as the credibility of the person delivering the advice. Sometimes you will receive conflicting feedback. Two weeks before the Athens Paralympics, two different coaches gave me conflicting feedback on my race dive. After clarifying, and on careful reflection, I discarded one lot of feedback. Not only was one of the coaches less experienced, he was also unable to see the dive clearly in the position he was in.

FOLLOW UP

On a National Programme there is often a considerable amount of information to disseminate to athletes, coaches and support crew, from age group and youth development through to senior elite.

As a National Programme employee, it is very easy to send an information mail out via e-mail to all programme participants and then automatically assume that they all:

- received it;
- read it;
- understood it; and
- implemented it.

You learn very quickly that this is not the case and that communication is a lot more than sending a mass e-mail. Our best responses have come from:

- individually personalizing the information;
- sending information that requires a response back; and
- following up mass e-mails with a personal call.

People always assume that my primary business is swimming because I am a swimming coach, but I can assure them that swimming is secondary. I am first and foremost in the communications business.

Lars Humer
Sports coach

THE LAST WORD

So remember: communication is an essential part of improving your personal best. Fortunately, it is easy to improve your communication skills. But don't make the mistake of thinking that communication is all about talking or writing: much of it, as we have seen, is non-verbal, and listening is a key skill. Sometimes saying nothing at all is best.

SEVEN

Going under?

Let me embrace thee, sour adversity,
For wise men say it is the wisest course.
William Shakespeare, *Henry VI, Part III*

Far better it is to dare mighty things, to win glorious
triumphs, even though chequered by failure, than to
take rank with those poor spirits who neither enjoy
much nor suffer much, because they live in the grey
twilight that knows not victory nor defeat.
Teddy Roosevelt

The greatest glory in living lies not in never falling,
but in rising every time we fall.
Nelson Mandela

WHEN THINGS GO BADLY

Two days before I was due to fly to Sydney for the 2000 Paralympic Games, my father unexpectedly died of a massive stroke. The following day I had to contact the British Paralympic Association and tell them that I wouldn't be able to make my flight out of the UK.

Suddenly, despite the years of preparation, I wasn't sure if I wanted to go to Sydney at all. I wanted to spend time with my brother Ian and Mum. But, as we waited for the day of the funeral, I gradually realized that cancelling my plans would have been the last thing that Dad would have wanted. In fact, he would have been furious with himself if he had become the reason for me missing out on the Paralympics. Even in his death I didn't want to upset Dad, so I contacted the British Paralympic Association again and they booked me on a late flight to Sydney.

Earlier in the week, when we met the funeral director, I had asked that they remove the ring that Dad had always worn. It was a simple gold ring and had been a present from Mum on his 21st birthday. It was the only jewellery that he had ever worn – he had given his wedding ring to Ian a couple of years earlier.

When the coffin was placed at the front of the crematorium, one of the coffin bearers turned to me and placed the ring in my hand. As we sang 'Eternal Father, Strong to Save', I turned Dad's ring over and over in my hand. I continued to do so during 'Love Divine, All Loves Excelling' the hymn that Mum and Dad had chosen for happier days – their wedding.

After the funeral was over, all of my father's friends came up to me and said, 'Bring back a gold for him, your Dad, the old fella.'

If it were that easy, everyone would win a gold medal, wouldn't they? I guess there are some people who don't know what else to say and that talking about swimming was least painful.

I couldn't believe that Dad had gone. He had always been there for me and in an instant he had gone. The only thing that comforted me was the fact that there was nothing left unsaid between us.

Knocked back

Sometimes, no matter how hard we try, things go badly. Something happens, whether it is because of our own actions, someone else's, the team's, or whether it is an event beyond our control.

The event itself and its apparent significance may bear no relation to the extent of the consequences. When the Scottish skier Alain Baxter used a Vick inhaler, he had no idea it would rob him of a bronze medal at the 2002 Winter Olympics in Salt Lake City. Baxter won the bronze for Great Britain in the slalom only to be stripped of his medal after it was found that the Vick inhaler he used for a blocked nose contained a banned substance – unlike the equivalent product in the UK.

When the space shuttle *Columbia* was launched in January 2003, a small piece of insulating foam fell off the fuel tank. It measured roughly 27 inches long and 18 inches wide, and weighed about two pounds. That small piece of foam indirectly caused the deaths of seven astronauts. It set the NASA space programme back by two years and cost the Agency over $1.4 billion (£750 million) in attempt to analyze and fix the problem.

In the cases of Alain Baxter and NASA, the setbacks were major ones. However, setbacks can be insignificant and still have a significant adverse effect on your performance.

You get up for work. Your cereal has run out. You are late for the train, the next train is cancelled – wrong kind of leaves. When you do get a train, there's no seat. You arrive at work late to find that your assistant is off sick. You have 150 e-mails waiting for you. The lunch meeting is cancelled, but you only find out after you have arrived. There's an unscheduled late meeting that means you miss the usual train home. The train you do catch gets in on time, but your mobile phone breaks down, the phone by the station is out of order, you haven't got any money on you and you left your credit card in the restaurant at the lunch appointment you didn't have. You walk home. It rains. When you get home, your partner greets you, as do the two dinner guests who are just on their way home. Your partner isn't smiling.

I'm sure many of you have been there, or close. How you react to the day's setbacks can have a huge impact on your performance. You can emerge from a day like this relatively unscathed or psychologically scarred for days.

How we deal with these personal setbacks often defines our character. Some people are naturally resilient, optimistic and forward-looking; they face up to setbacks, deal with them and move on. Many of us, however, stumble at some point. We deny, we avoid, we hide and we get stuck.

CHEWING IT OVER

There are big gender differences over how we perceive the world and how we deal with setbacks.

Women tend to be more pessimistic than men. In the Gallup International Voice of the People survey for the World Economic Forum, over 43,000 citizens in more than

50 countries across the globe were interviewed. Women were more pessimistic than men on the security of their country, the country's economic prospects, their family's economic prosperity, whether the next generation will be safer or less safe than existing generations, and the economic prospects of the next generation. Women are also more likely to worry and dwell on setbacks.

Susan Nolen-Hoeksema is professor of psychology at Yale University. Her specialist area of research is depression in women; in particular, she has identified a particular style of thinking called 'rumination' that women tend to adopt more often than men.

Ruminating is a tendency to respond to distress by focusing on the causes and consequences of problems without getting into a problem-solving and 'taking action' mode. Those people who tend to ruminate are prone to more severe and prolonged periods of depression. They are also more prone to behave in an impulsive and escapist way, resorting to bingeing on food and drink. Finally, rumination exacerbates negative thinking and acts as a barrier to good problem-solving.

According to Nolen-Hoeksema, we all ruminate from time to time and to a certain degree. Most of us pull ourselves out of our ruminations; however, some do not. With them it becomes a self-fuelling spiral of worry. These ruminators get deeper and deeper into a rut.

Nolen-Hoeksema's research has revealed that, when it comes to coping with difficult situations, in general 'women think and men drink'.

Like most other things in life, you can improve the way you cope with setbacks. How? By understanding a little bit about what is involved, identifying the common behaviour patterns, learning how to avoid them or deal with them and, in a more general way, learning how to deal with stress.

Stress is a common result of setbacks, major or minor – although positive events can also cause stress. Either way, learning to deal with stress is a very important skill. You can't change the way you behave in the face of a setback overnight, but you can, as I have done, learn to recognize the signs of stress, what happens – and take action to combat it.

DEALING WITH SETBACKS

Injuries have made me grasp opportunities three times harder. I had various injuries throughout my career, but each time I came back more hungry. I also learnt some other important lessons through injuries. At a young age I was climbing unprotected and fell, breaking both my femurs. It gave me a rude awakening but made me a far better climber. It made me understand the consequences of my actions.

John Dunne
Professional climber

STRESS – WHAT IS IT?

Stress is a response, or range of responses, to a disruption of our normal state caused by internal or external factors.

Homeostasis is the state of dynamic balance our body is maintained in. When internal or external factors upset that balance, the body adjusts and adapts to maintain balance. Sometimes, however, its normal responses are not enough to restore balance – in which case, the stress response kicks in.

The full-blown stress response – often described as the 'fight or flight' response – is a very important mechanism. It helps us to deal with a threat to our well-being.

The general adaptation syndrome, identified by the Austrian physician Hans Selye in the 1920s, involves three stages: alarm, resistance, exhaustion. In the first stage, you are exposed to a stimulus that you are not adapted to, such as a mugger after your mobile. You briefly go into shock before your hormones kick in to counter the shock. You then adapt to the stressor. If the stressor remains for a length of time, however, your body may be unable to continue to cope with the stressor, and you may become fatigued and vulnerable to illness. This is because when your body's resources are marshalled to deal with the stressor, they are unavailable for duty elsewhere – fighting off 'flu bugs, for instance.

The stress response is fine for dealing with sudden threats such as a mugger – it gets you ready to run or fight. Although, truthfully, it is probably better to hand over your mobile. Where the stress response is less useful is in cases where there is a prolonged low-level challenge to the homeostasis.

When the mugger appears, we are aware of our heart beating faster, muscles tensing, breath quickening, plus the feeling of adrenaline coursing around our body. With low-level stress, the effects are sub-clinical: undetected for the most part, yet still affecting the body. Pile the workload up and add in an unreliable transport system and the body reacts to the stressors and goes on reacting.

Another way of thinking about stress is to look at it in terms of the demands made of you and the resources that you have available to deal with those demands. The demand might be physical or psychological. If you have insufficient resources to meet the demand, you will feel stressed. If you don't have enough money to pay the mortgage, you will feel stressed. If you don't have the right skills or knowledge to perform a task at work, you will feel stressed.

THE SCIENCE OF STRESS

Nervous system

The stress response involves the part of the nervous system that controls automatic activity within the body – the autonomic nervous system (as opposed to the voluntary system).

The autonomic nervous system (ANS) is made up of the sympathetic and parasympathetic systems. The sympathetic system prepares the body for action by stimulating the secretion of hormones. The parasympathetic system maintains and regulates the body at rest.

Hormones

The main hormones involved in the response to physical and emotional stress are secreted by the adrenal glands next to the kidneys. They are adrenaline, noradrenaline and cortisol.

Adrenaline and noradrenaline affect receptors throughout the body causing the heart to beat faster, blood vessels to dilate and freeing up glucose to be burned up by muscles.

Cortisol is secreted by the adrenal glands in response to the production of cortiocotropin-releasing hormone

(CRH) in the brain. The hormone breaks down muscle protein and releases amino acids into the bloodstream. The liver uses these amino acids to synthesize glucose, which provides energy for the brain. At the same time, cortisol stimulates the production of fatty acids from fat cells for the muscles to use as energy.

Other responses

As well as the effects of the hormones secreted by the adrenal glands, there are other reactions taking place in the body during periods of stress. Endorphins help suppress pain and the digestive system slows down, allowing blood to be diverted to more important parts of the body.

Prolonged stress

All the body's stress reactions described above are designed to facilitate action. If there is no action, then the release of hormones designed to help the body survive can harm it instead. If glucose is produced but not used, it can upset blood sugar levels and lead to problems such as diabetes and anxiety. Too much cortisol has been associated with poor immune system response, cardiovascular problems, osteoporosis and other health problems.

Are you stressed?

Recognizing the signs of stress is vital. The earlier you can detect stress and its causes, the sooner you can start to deal with it. Stress affects us physically, psychologically, emotionally and behaviourally.

Physical signs include sleep problems, changes in the menstrual cycle, headaches, chest pain and palpitations, weight loss or gain, skin problems, ulcers, and irritable bowel syndrome.

Psychological signs include negative thinking, ruminating, depression and negative self-talk.

Behavioural and emotional signs include mood swings, a lack of enthusiasm, anger, guilt, irritability, feeling helpless, low self-esteem, poor concentration, lack of relaxation, poor time management, eating disorders, binge-drinking, suppression of sexual appetite, and withdrawal and anti-social behaviour.

STRESS BUSTING

If stress is bad for us, then obviously the less stressed we are the better. It may be impossible for most of us to eliminate stress completely from our lives, but we can make a start.

Destressing

The best way to deal with stress is to remove the stressor – whatever is causing the stress. This may mean actual physical removal, or dealing with the stressor so that it no longer exists. So if you are a mother of a teenage son who insists on playing the drums in his room, you could put them in the back of the car and donate them to the local charity shop when he goes out, doing whatever teenagers do. Alternatively you could soundproof his room – requiring an inner skin of plasterboard and lot of sand, if you're interested.

However, not all stressors are easily removed. The stressor may not be under your control. Maybe it is the neighbour's loud music that is causing you stress. In this case, break down the process of dealing with the stress into a series of steps. Then tackle each in turn.

In the case of the neighbour's music, first you would contact the neighbour and attempt to agree a solution that you are both happy with. If you fail to reach agreement, or even enter into discussions, you may need to compile evidence over a period of time and then contact the local authority; or it may be worth contacting the local authority straight away. Finally, you must have the conviction to see the process through. With this situation, as with many others, assertiveness is important.

In some cases, stress is caused by the absence rather than the presence of something, as in the case of the loss of someone or something you care about. In these cases, you can't physically remove the stressor, and you can't run away from it. You must deal with it on a psychological level.

THE BIG DAY

Ask a group of people what the biggest day of their lives was, and many will mention either the birth of their children or their wedding day. Both can be extremely stressful occasions. Running my wedding venue – which involves guaranteeing the success and smooth running of, on average, 50 weddings a year – means I incur a great deal of stress as clients depend on me to ensure that their special day lives up to their hopes and dreams.

Most couples plan a wedding months, if not years, in advance, and can spend hours discussing every detail. The pressure this puts on me can be immense. When the business was first up and running I was not so aware of the enormity of what I had taken on. Now I realize that, ultimately, the success of each wedding depends on me. Once I had realized this, I knew I needed some coping strategies to ease the demands being made upon me.

To build confidence, I considered the following things:

- Plan in advance – anxieties are dealt with early on in a non-stressful state.
- Have a first-class team.
- Focus on the things that matter. I focus on ensuring the happiness and state of mind of the bride and groom and their respective parents. If they are happy and relaxed, so should the guests be.
- Continue to strive to improve, in my case improving the venue and enhancing its uniqueness.

William Deeley
Managing Director of the Tythe Barn

Take control

Stress is often caused by being in situations where you feel unable to control events. By taking control of your life, you can help eliminate stress.

You can start in small ways. For example, you can eliminate ruminating by limiting yourself to a set time – five minutes, say – when considering problems. After this time, you should be thinking about what you need to do to deal with the problem and then putting a problem-solving plan into action, rather than still focusing on the causes and consequences of the problem.

Assertiveness is another area where you can take control of your life. If you find yourself in situations where you are unable to get your point of view across, are unable to raise issues for fear of confrontation or shy away from verbal conflict, then you will benefit from becoming more assertive.

Assertiveness is about external attitude and having the confidence to express your views. To do this, you need to have a strong sense of self-worth. You have as much right as others to express yourself.

If you are assertive, you will be able to:

- communicate without aggression;
- avoid agreeing or disagreeing with others just to please them;
- stick up for yourself;
- defend your position,
- handle conflict when it occurs; and
- negotiate.

People who are unable to stick up for themselves and who cannot express their opinions behave in a passive way when it comes to communicating with others. They might, for example, be sarcastic, resentful, or – as is often the case – silent.

Body language

If you want to be assertive, you need to focus on a number of things. For example, don't send out a 'victim' body language signal: hunched over or avoiding eye contact. And don't send out an aggressive signal: clenched fists, glaring or invading personal space. Instead, have an upright stance with an open posture and be relaxed, with your hands open and making good eye contact.

Communication

I have talked about the importance of good communication and it is especially true if you want to be assertive. You must be able to sum up a given situation, express your feelings and your needs as well as listening to the feelings and needs of others. You will need to communicate calmly and clearly. Stick to the point, clarify any points you are unclear on and be prepared to have a Plan B or C where the outcomes are acceptable to you.

You must relate things to the way you feel and think. Use language such as 'I think', 'I feel', 'This is how I see things', 'In my opinion', 'I want' or 'I need'. Even if you are ascertaining how the other person feels, relate it to how you feel: 'I think ..., what do *you* think?' or 'I feel ..., how do *you* feel?'

Try to avoid blaming language such as 'You shouldn't' or 'It's your fault'.

In international politics, when diplomacy doesn't work countries go to war. In many people's minds, being assertive involves an underlying implicit threat of aggression and violence. *You* might be very good at being assertive and excellent at communicating – but what if the person you are dealing with isn't?

Some people who are unable to communicate will resort to aggression in order to preserve their self-esteem. It is not always easy to tell who these people are and it's not always easy to defuse such a situation, which means that to be truly confident in a potentially confrontational situation it is good to know how to defend yourself from physical attack.

There are many different types of personal defence classes and it is worth considering taking some. The world shouldn't be like this, but there is no harm in being pragmatic – being prepared helps.

Protect against stress

It is not always possible to remove stressors. In these cases it is sometimes better to remove yourself. There may be a temptation to see stress situations as battles to be won – this is especially true if other people, such as neighbours, colleagues or employers are involved. Ultimately, however, you must weigh up the preservation of self-esteem from waging the battle against the physical and psychological detrimental effects.

There will always be circumstances, however, when you cannot remove the stressor or yourself. Work is a good example. You may have a very heavy workload combined with impossible deadlines; while it is possible to take some steps at work to ease the situation, it may not be possible to remove it entirely. You could walk away from the job, but you may have a family to support or a mortgage to pay – or both.

Perhaps the best you can do is to follow some of these tips, which should help protect you against the effects of stress.

ORDINARY PEOPLE, EXTRAORDINARY LIVES

In April 2003, 27-year-old Aron Ralston was climbing in Canyonlands National Park in Utah. Whilst trying to get past a large boulder wedged between the narrow canyon walls, the perfectly balanced 800lb rock shifted several feet, pinning his right arm.

Ralston tried everything to move the boulder, but he couldn't. He tried to chip away at the rock with a multi-tool, but to no avail. After four days he ran out of food and, more importantly, water. On the fifth day he recorded a video message to his parents and etched his name and birth date into the canyon wall.

The following day, Ralston had a vision of a three-year-old boy running across a sunlit floor to be scooped up by a one-armed man. He believed it was a vision of his future son and decided it was time for drastic action. He decided to amputate his right arm below the elbow using the knife blade on his multi-tool. But first, because his knife wasn't sharp enough to get through the bone, he had to force his arm against the boulder to break the radius and ulna. He then amputated his right arm below the elbow.

His survival still wasn't assured, however. He rigged anchors and fixed a rope then let himself nearly 70-feet down to the bottom of the canyon. Leaving his rope hanging, he hiked five miles downstream where he encountered a Dutch family on vacation who helped him call in a rescue helicopter.

Exercise

The benefits of exercise are well proven: it improves fitness and health. But not just any exercise – it is simply not true that *any* exercise is better than none. Having failed to venture from your armchair for five years, signing up for a marathon with two weeks' notice is not a good idea. And, despite the occasional media report suggesting otherwise, the following do not constitute exercise in any beneficial sense:

• walking 100 yards to the shops;

- walking to work (if the walking element involves getting on and off a train and into a taxi);
- clubbing once a week (where the clubbing involves standing still and drinking lots of alcohol); and
- climbing the stairs to bed.

To get some benefits, your exercise should be regular, enjoyable if possible, and structured. Ideally it should be a mixture of cardiovascular, core body control and strength exercise. And, if you have been inactive for a long period, you should start gradually.

It may not sound so macho in the gym, but there can be gain without pain. For example, if your exercise target is to try to maintain or lose weight, as opposed to breaking the marathon world record, you don't need to drive yourself into the ground. The right level of exercise to begin with is where you are slightly out of breath but are still able to talk to someone. If you can exercise for 20–30 minutes five times a week then you will benefit considerably.

Probably the biggest issue when it comes to taking exercise is time. If you are going to exercise regularly, you will need to create time for it. Finding a regular slot helps. If you choose an activity you enjoy, then you are more likely to stick to the time. This is also true if someone else is involved. If you go running on your own, it is easy to miss a session. If you play badminton or tennis, it is harder to let the other person down. Either way, you will need to motivate yourself at some point – in which case, see Chapter 4. One easy way of getting regular exercise is to go for a brisk walk with a friend several times a week. And that is not a *double entendre* – I do mean 'walk'.

EXERCISE: CAN YOU AFFORD NOT TO?

A few exercise facts:

- The UK government recommends exercising for 30 minutes, five times a week.
- Exercise can reduce the risk of cardiovascular disease, some cancers, strokes and obesity.
- Physical inactivity costs England £20 billion a year.
- A 10% increase in physical activity would save about 6000 out of 54,000 lives lost prematurely due to lack of physical exercise each year. That's a saving £500,000 in healthcare and other associated costs.

Diet

Stress and diet are connected in several ways. A good diet keeps us healthy and protects us against stress. Stress, however, often affects the way we eat. It may cause us to miss lunch breaks, snack at work or snatch something to eat on the move. It may also cause us to eat for comfort to relieve the stress or lose weight through stress-related loss of appetite.

My diet was always determined by the amount of energy I needed. During the periods of hardest training, I would eat approximately 6000 calories each day. If I didn't do that, then my energy levels would drop and my weight decrease. However, eating that much is hard work: when I was stressed there were times I couldn't manage it and that would have a direct effect on my ability to train.

FOOD FOR THOUGHT

Is the key to get a balance between calories taken in and calories expended?
Yes. It is a simple equation:

Energy in = energy out: weight stable.
Energy in > energy out: weight gain.
Energy in < energy out: weight loss.

Increasingly in the UK, fewer people are getting the balance right due to either eating too much or not exercising enough, or probably a combination of the two – and we are getting fatter!

We have to eat the right proportions of the various food groups at the right time. What are those proportions? What is the timing?
The average British diet contains 40% of the energy from carbohydrate (CHO), 40% from fat and 20% from protein.

For a healthy diet, the government recommends 50% of the energy from CHO, 30% from fat and 20% from protein.

For an athlete, it should be at least 60% from CHO, 25% from fat and 15% from protein. On the face of it, this looks like the athlete will be getting less protein than the non-athlete, but an athlete's energy intake is higher than the average person so the total grams of protein will be about the same or even more.

It is better to spread food out evenly between the three meals a day rather than try to eat it all at one meal – this helps keep the metabolism up and can utilize nutrients better.

Everyone needs to eat as wide a variety of foods as possible to ensure they are getting enough vitamins and minerals. No single food contains all of the vitamins and minerals we need: therefore, the wider the variety, the more likely it is that people will get all the nutrients required.

For people who exercise a lot, what are the key principles for a healthy diet?
They are a person first and an athlete second – so they should be trying to have everything a person needs and then some!

This is obviously very general and there will be a great deal of individual variation, which is why it is a good idea to see a sports dietician for more detailed advice.

They need to:

- have high-CHO, low-fat, moderate-protein meals every day, not just on training or competition days.
- drink at least two litres of fluid per day and extra during training. They should:
  - monitor the colour of their urine to determine whether they need to drink more during the day (ignoring the first pee in the morning);
  - weigh themselves before and after exercise to determine whether they need to drink more during exercise, aiming to lose no more than 1% of their body weight during exercise;
  - drink 1.5 times the weight lost to regain full hydration – 1.5 litres for every kilo lost.
- eat a high-CHO, low-fat snack/meal within 30 minutes of finishing exercise, aiming for 1g of CHO per kilogram in body weight. This usually means 50–100g of CHO – one or two things from Table 7.1.

Table 7.1 Table of foods which contain approximately 50g carbohydrate

Food	Approximate weight	Household measure
Bread, large loaf, medium sliced	100g	3 slices
Bread, large loaf, thick sliced	100g	2 slices
Fruit scone	100g	2 scones
Malt loaf	100g	2 slices
Bananas	400g	2 large
Raisins/sultanas	70g	3 heaped tablespoons
Dried apricots	125g	15–20 apricots
Nutrigrain bars	65g	2 bars
Cereal bars		2–3 – go for lowest fat
Swiss roll	90g	3 slices
Fig rolls	70g	4–5 biscuits
Jaffa Cakes	60g	6 biscuits
Gingernuts	80g	8 biscuits
Plain digestives	75g	5 biscuits
Iced Gems	60g	2 bags
Boiled sweets	60g	
Liquorice Allsorts	75g	
Fruit Pastilles	80g	2 tubes
Sports drink containing 6g CHO per 100ml	850ml	

- have one rest day a week, which should be used to rest and eat high-CHO, low-fat foods to get glycogen stores completely full.

So they need to do this as well as what follows.

How does this differ for healthy everyday people?
- Eat a wide variety of food.
- Eat at least five portions of fruit and vegetables a day.
- Spread food out throughout the day – eat breakfast.
- Stay in energy balance. If you need to lose weight, you need to be in negative energy balance; if you need to gain weight, you need to be in positive energy balance – this applies to athletes too.
- Drink at least two litres of fluid a day – and it wouldn't hurt to monitor urine colour either

For people who are trying to lose weight, is it better not to refuel directly after exercise?
No, they need to refuel too, but they need to have it counted in their total energy allowance for the day. If they eat high-CHO, low-fat food after exercise, then that will be used to fill their glycogen stores first and will not turn to fat – they need to refuel just like everyone else, or their stores won't be full in time for the next session. Glycogen can be replaced quickest in the first two hours after exercise.

Jeanie Baker
Sports dietician

Sleep

Research shows us that adequate sleep is essential for good health. Sleep deprivation has been linked to all kinds of unpleasant ailments: according to various studies, if we are sleep-deprived we are more likely to suffer heart attacks, die earlier, get diabetes, be paranoid, become obese, have high blood pressure and experience hallucinations. We are also likely to fall asleep at the desk, on the sofa or at the wheel of a car. In the US, the National Highway Traffic Safety Administration estimates that driver fatigue accounts for 100,000 motor vehicle accidents and 1500 deaths each year. With complete sleep deprivation, the outlook is grim. Rats deprived of all sleep die after about three weeks.

Fortunately, if we go without sleep, we can catch up. Being deprived of sleep is like getting overdrawn at the bank: we can make a deposit a little later – maybe at the weekend – to get back into the black. Unlike the bank, we do not even have to pay in as much sleep as we were deprived of. Studies suggest we only need to make up about 30%.

It is a better idea to get enough sleep to start with, though. The question is: what is an adequate amount of sleep? An English proverb states 'Six hours sleep for a man, seven for a woman and eight for a fool.' According to US sleep researchers, we are better off as fools. They estimate that adults need between seven and eight hours sleep per night on average.[1] In the UK, the Sleep Research Centre at Loughborough puts the figure a little more conservatively at not less than six hours. Albert Einstein needed more than nine hours; Thomas Edison fewer than six. I can go several days with six hours' sleep, but

---

[1] http://www.ninds.nih.gov/disorders/brain_basics/understanding_sleep.htm

then will be a far happier person if I can then back that up with a couple of nights with eight hours. Women apparently sleep 15 minutes more than men on average.[2]

If you have trouble getting off to sleep at night, you are in good company. In the US, 40 million people suffer from chronic long-term sleep disorders each year – sleep disorders that cause excessive daytime sleepiness – with an extra 20 million having occasional sleeping problems. In the UK, for example, about 2% of the population (or approximately 300,000 people) suffer from sleep apnoea, where the airway is intermittently blocked during sleep, causing the sufferer to continually wake up.

Help is at hand, however. The Sleep Research Centre at Loughborough has some useful tips for improving your chance of getting a good night's sleep:[3]

- no caffeine in the evening;
- have a relaxing, if mundane, bedtime routine;
- don't go to bed until you feel sleepy;
- avoid too much mind stimulation in the bedroom – no TV or radio;
- if you don't get to sleep fairly swiftly, get up and do something distracting but not stimulating – ironing, perhaps – and, when you get sleepy, go back to bed;
- don't clock-watch;
- if you have difficulty sleeping one night, you will probably make up for it the next; and
- try to get up at the same time every morning – it helps to set your natural body clock.

Relaxation techniques can also aid sleep and fight off stress.

---

[2] Sleep Research Laboratory at Loughborough University

[3] www.lboro.ac.uk/departments/hu/groups/sleep

The visualization technique I practised before I went to Atlanta would help me relax as I was going to sleep. It is almost a type of meditation and would ensure I fell asleep quickly. I used a similar process when I was having my chemotherapy. It was a particularly stressful time and I would think about what I planned to do when it was all over – swimming, skiing and spending time with my friends. All of these things would help me relax, sleep and pass the time as painlessly as possible. For more on these techniques, see Chapter 10.

Family and social life

When we are stressed, we often become withdrawn. Family and social life suffer. Ironically it is this kind of social contact that can help alleviate stress. Therefore it is a good idea if you plan time for family, friends and social activities.

Hobbies and other non-work-related activity are also very useful in fighting stress. If you don't already have one, it really is worth taking one up, whether it is stamp collecting, sky diving or sailing.

When I'm rock climbing, for example, I rarely think of work and for that period of time, no matter how brief, I'm free of work-related stress. There *is* the stress of falling off a cliff to contend with, of course!

Similarly, I have a friend who goes fishing. Not because he catches much – he is full of 'the one that got away' tales – but more to forget about work and other worries of the world.

Shopping therapy is another way of relieving stress – so long as you have adequate financial resources, and are not creating another source of stress.

DEALING WITH STRESS

Being a cancer doctor, treating children and young people can be very stressful. But getting to know the young person, what they like to do outside hospital, what excites them and so on, makes it easier, not harder, to treat them – not focusing on the disease but the whole person. I particularly like to get people to tell me jokes, draw a picture or tell me a story – I guess it is distraction for both of us! My jokes are corny, mainly because I get them from the books I have received from patients over the years. Only one member of our team has worse jokes – our outreach sister who has been practising since 1970, as long as I have.

Looking back to the early 1970s is helpful too. Outcomes were so awful then that nowadays things don't look so bad, especially as we can control symptoms better now. At least once a year I need to escape completely, away from work, phones, TV and so on, and go walking in the Norwegian mountains, close to nature and away from everyone except my wife – my partner, confidant and supporter for 35+ years.

Professor in Paediatric Oncology

FUNNY BONE

I'm lying in my hospital room. It's not even 24 hours since my leg was amputated. As I come round, I feel a pressing need. My bladder feels like a ten-pin bowling ball. I push the buzzer to call for the nurse.

'Are you all right, Marc?'

'I'm busting for a pee. Can you give me a hand to the loo?'

'Hold on. I will be right back.'

She disappears and I try not to think about it. Then, a couple of minutes later, she comes back. But she is not alone – she has brought with her another nurse and Sister Benedict, the octogenarian nun who is in charge of my ward.

'I only need to go for a wee,' I say, a little perplexed at the entourage. 'I just need some help to the loo.'

'You can't get out of bed,' Sister Benedict says. 'We will have to help you.'

The two nurses help me to sit up and then sit themselves down beside me, each with their arms looped through mine. Sister Benedict then drops to her knees in front of me. In her hand is a plastic urine bottle. She motions for me to place myself in the neck of the bottle, which I do, and then we all wait: me, the two nurses, and the nun. And wait.

Have you have ever had a problem going to the loo in a public toilet? I imagine this is less of an issue for a woman – you get your own private space. But for men it's different. You enter a public toilet and quickly glance around, looking for the urinal that is furthest away from anyone else. But often, you still have to stand next to someone. The first few moments of not being able to pee are OK – after all, you have only just got there. You look straight ahead. Always straight ahead, never to the side. The person next to you finishes and this instils in you a hope that you might be able to manage it soon, but he is replaced instantly by someone else. You still can't go. What do you do? Do you hang in there and keep trying, or pretend you finished a while ago?

It's a dilemma many men are familiar with. And, if you have ever been in that situation, you will know how it feels. This was much, much, worse.

I could feel the nurses' hands lightly gripping my upper arms; they were willing me on. I looked at Sister Benedict her gaze intently fixed on the task at hand as she gently held the plastic bottle. Ask yourself, could you pee under such duress? Now that is what I call a gargantuan challenge. Forget the goal of trying to win a gold medal – it was nothing, a mere trifle, compared with this. Climbing Cotopaxi? A walk in the park. This task was hardcore. So how did I measure up to the challenge?

'Er … I'm sorry, everyone, but I don't think I need to go now … actually … thanks.'

No matter how bad things get, I have always tried to see the funny side of a situation. Even in intensely stressful environments, it is sometimes possible to smile and reduce the tension in some way. In some of my darkest moments during the series of chemo treatments I managed to find something to laugh at and someone to laugh with.

So how did I cope with what were very stressful situations for me? As well as I could – and with a smile.

EIGHT

A helping hand

Setting an example is not the main means of
influencing another, it is the only means.
Albert Einstein

I think it's an honour to be a role model to one person or
maybe more than that. If you are given a chance to be a
role model, I think you should always take it because you
can influence a person's life in a positive light, and that's
what I want to do. That's what it's all about.
Tiger Woods

A SHINING EXAMPLE

I have supported the work of the Teenage Cancer Trust for some time now. Occasionally they ask if I would visit young people in hospital to offer understanding and perhaps inspiration.

As you know, where cancer is concerned, my philosophy has been that it doesn't have to be a life sentence. You can beat it – life can get better. But obviously not everyone does get better.

I once visited a young 12-year-old boy. We really connected. In some ways, he reminded me of myself. When we first met, he didn't know where the cancer was going to take him, but, like me, he was committed to being as positive as he could be about his situation.

Then, one day, he did know. He wasn't going to live to see the next Christmas. I didn't know what to say to him for a while. What could I do? I skirted around the issue until I realized that was exactly what I hated when people did it to me. So I asked him what he wanted to do in the time he had left. He wanted to spend as much time as he could with his brother, and he wanted to make up with a school friend with whom he had had a disagreement over nothing. I don't know if I helped him in anyway. I was almost embarrassed to be there – as though I was taunting him with the fact I had survived and he was going to die. All I could do was be the best friend that I could be.

Then there was John Waters. There I was, happily swimming up and down the pool, when I became aware of someone swimming directly behind me. I was in my usual training lane at the Barnet Copthall swimming pool and there appeared to be an unexpected addition to my training partners. In fact, he was so close to me, his hands kept tapping my foot. Swimming bad manners is what it was.

At the next rest interval, I asked if he would like to go in front of me. 'Oh no I'm fine just here thanks,' he said in an East Coast American accent. It turned out to be the start of an excellent period of training. John had temporarily moved to London from Connecticut. If he had been British he would have been one of the fastest male swimmers in Great Britain for his age. As it was, he was just happy to train with us.

John seemed to be on a constant quest to improve. One moment he would be quizzing me and the other world-class swimmers about some training technique; the next, he would be improving his Italian, chatting with some of the international visitors we used to get at swimming club.

He loved to pick up on any colloquial English that I used. I once used the word 'comfy' instead of 'comfortable' and our standard training phrase became 'keep it comfy', regardless of how painful the training session was.

He was a great training partner and a fine example of how to embrace all aspects of life.

At the time I was 26 years old and John was 14.

John, subsequently, went on to graduate from Stanford University and narrowly miss out on a place in the US swim team that competed at the 2000 Sydney Olympics. He is now studying pre-medical core in preparation for medical school and is hoping to become a surgeon one day. I have no doubt that he will achieve that.

ROLE MODELS: WHAT ARE THEY?

Role models are people who possess qualities and abilities that we admire, and would like to have. They show us what is possible and motivate us to achieve greater things.

Over the years I have had several role models, but only a few have stood the test of time. Like most children, my earliest role models were influenced by the media – celebrity athletes, pop stars and footballers. These were the people I idolized and wanted to emulate.

In hindsight, I realize that the value of these role models was very limited. Their fame subsided and their achievements faded. Sometimes the media unearthed a more unhealthy side to their character. But there were some role models whose long-term effects on me have been profoundly life-changing.

Some I found in unexpected places, such as the Barnet Copthall pool. John Waters was a great role model for me. We met at a time when I was finding it very difficult to train hard every day for a competition that was over a year away. John helped me to realize that, at that point at least, it was more important to enjoy the process than focus on the outcome. If I enjoyed the process of training, the outcome was more likely to be a successful one.

I found other role models where most of us, if we are lucky, should expect to find them. They are the people who help you form your overall outlook on life. They provide you with your moral markers from which all else is measured. They are, of course, your parents.

Parents as role models

A 2003 survey by Harris Interactive on behalf of Gillette revealed that nearly half of the women surveyed looked to their mothers as their role model. In another survey, 46% of teenagers said their role model is not a pop icon or a sports star, but a family member. And there are many more that don't refer to their parents or other family members as role models but still see them as such. Research also suggests that adolescents who have positive role models have higher self-esteem and are more likely to do well in school.

If you are a parent, you have an incredible influence on your children. By setting a good example, you can help your child make healthy choices in their life. Even when you think that they aren't listening or paying attention, they are picking up on your verbal and non-verbal communications. Remember: your values and opinions, and the example you give, greatly affect your child's development.

HOW DO YOU MEASURE UP?

Ask yourself these questions and see if you are being the best role model you can be for your child:

1. Would you like to see your child acting like you?
One of the easiest and fastest ways for a child to learn is by imitating. If you demonstrate respect for yourself, those around you and the environment, it is more likely your child will do the same.

2. Do you explain your values to your child?
Before you can explain your values to children, you may need to reflect on what your values are and why you hold them. Explaining to your child how and why you have your values will encourage them to adopt similar values.

3. Do you deal with emotional issues and stress in a healthy way?

Coping with stresses and emotional anxiety is part of everybody's life. Are you ready to engage in an open dialogue with your children so that they can learn how to deal with these battles?

4. Do you allow your children to see that life can be a combination of both success and failure?

Help your children to realize that things don't always go to plan. Sometimes a change in approach and behaviour is required if you are to continue to work towards your goals.

5. Do you spend quality time with your family?

There is no substitute for spending time together with your family. It is not always easy, but sharing experiences is an excellent way of showing someone you care. Listening to their hopes and concerns demonstrates a genuine interest in their life. If you are able to listen to them, they are far more likely to turn to you when they need advice.

6. Are you interested in your child's school education and extra curricular activities?

Showing an interest in your child's life away from home encourages them to participate more, and gives you the opportunity to help them develop.

My father, my hero

My first role model was my father. His passion, optimism, drive and caring nature still influence me today. He guided and nurtured me, and moulded me into the person I am today. He taught me to swim, and encouraged me to continue swimming.

We lived in a small village called North Thoresby, just outside Grimsby in the north-east of England. The local pool, Scartho Baths, was a 20-minute journey into town. It was a cavernous building, or so it seemed to me when I was four.

I remember standing on the cold changing room floor in nothing but my tiny swimming trunks, my arms folded across my chest, hugging my shoulders, as my dad took off his shoes and socks and rolled up his trouser legs.

Taking my hand, he led me to the hatch where we handed over a basket containing my clothes and dad's shoes and socks. In return we got a safety pin with a little numbered aluminium disk attached to it. Dad showed me how to attach the pin to the flimsy material of my trunks and we made our way back through the changing room.

He stepped into the footbath.

'Come on, then.'

I stepped into the cold murky water. It came to just below my knees. It smelled of disinfectant, but I couldn't believe it was clean. Thousands of feet must have passed through it since it was last changed. With Dad almost lifting me out of the water by my hand, we waded through and out onto the poolside.

The swimming pool was alive with people. Their shouts and screams, a mixture of excitement and fear, echoed around the hard tiled surface. There were groups of children huddled by the side wall, waiting for instructions. Some toppled in from diving boards of various heights. Others were in the pool. Large ladies in tight white tennis shirts and flip-flops leant over the water holding broomsticks, which they waved like giant wands.

'What are they doing with those sticks?' I asked.

'Oh, they're just holding them above the water so that if the children in the water can't swim any more, they can hold on to them. You don't need to worry about that. You won't need them.'

I was there to try for my first swimming badge. Dad had already taught me to swim, but getting a badge would be the proof. He went to talk to one of the ladies with the sticks. Then they both came over to where I was stood shivering.

'Are you going to try for your ten-metre badge, then?' she said. I just nodded.

'If you swim one width you will get your ten-metre badge. You can use any stroke you like and you can change the stroke if you get tired, but you mustn't walk on the bottom, stop, or hold onto the side. If you do, you won't get your badge. Do you understand?'

'All you have to do is swim across the width,' said Dad squatting down so that his face was level with mine. 'You can do that, can't you?'

'Yeah. I think so.'

'Good lad. In you jump.'

I sat on the edge of the pool and slid into the water. My feet couldn't reach the bottom. I started to swim, a kind of breaststroke-cum-doggy paddle.

'Good lad. That's it.' Dad walked along the edge next to me. 'Keep going. Good lad.'

The far side of the pool gradually came closer and closer. Dad was kneeling in front of me calling me forward.

'That's it, that's it! Almost there!'

I was within two or three strokes of the side now.

'Brilliant! Now turn around and swim back again.'

That was a bit of a surprise. I was sure he said once across the pool. But it was no time to argue. So I just did as I was told. I turned around and started to swim back.

'Great!' Dad was calling. 'You can do it!' I could see two wet patches on the knees of his best business suit where he had knelt down to urge me on.

'This isn't too bad,' I thought to myself. 'Just don't ask me to go back again.'

'Almost there! Great! You did it!' I grabbed the trough where the water overflowed at the end of the pool and Dad knelt down and ruffled my hair as I clung on to the edge. 'Well done, son.' He gripped me by the top of my arms and hauled me out onto the side again.

'I am dead proud of you, mate,' Dad said to me as he towelled my hair dry. 'Of all the things you will ever do in a swimming pool, that's the most important badge you will ever get. That badge means you can swim.'

Enthusiastically, he continued. 'When I was in the air sea rescue, sometimes I had to be lowered down on a winch to rescue people. Other times I would jump into the sea with all my diving kit on and help people who couldn't swim anymore. So you getting your swimming badges makes me feel really proud. Swimming is my sport.'

In the foyer, Dad paid some money to the man behind the counter who took two little oval badges out of a small Tupperware box and handed them over. Dad placed them in my hands. They were small ovals of cloth designed to be sewn onto a tracksuit. The ten-metre badge was purple and the 25-metre one green. In the centre were the words 'Distance Award', an embroidered man swimming butterfly and the distance. Between my Dad and me, it was difficult to tell who had the bigger grin.

ROLE MODELS AND MENTORS

I have a few role models for different reasons and I still look up to them now:

- Jesse Owens and Martin Luther King. Both achieved so much in adverse situations – their history speaks for itself.

- My sister. Despite the ten-year age gap, I wanted to be like my sister. She was an athlete but had to give it up due to injury. A lover of athletics herself, she has always encouraged me on and off the track. She brought me up to be confident, believe in myself, try not to have regrets and she always said that I should enjoy life the best I can.

- My parents. Being Afro-Caribbean in the UK, they had tough times in the 1960s, and I am proud that they came through it with true resilience. They taught me to be strong-minded and to work hard at what I want to achieve – and that anything is possible.

- Miss Hughes, my primary school teacher. She introduced athletics to me. She would always say to focus on something straight ahead, run towards it as fast as I can and 'be determined'. I will always remember that!

- Ayo Falola, my coach. He has taught me patience and commitment, and has given me tough love. Sometimes I don't appreciate the tough love, but it has helped me become stronger mentally and physically over the years he has coached me. He always says 'Aim high and anything else is a bonus'.

Donna Fraser
Olympic athlete

Multiple role models

My experiences with the 12-year-old boy and John made me realize that there are role models all around us. Both, in their own way, were role models for me. Both taught me something about how I should lead my life. In fact, I have had many role models. Some were all-round life role models, others were role models for specific issues I needed guidance on, whether it was sport, business or social responsibility. The key thing is that I haven't had to look far. Within a comparatively small circle of acquaintances, I have found people who can inspire and guide me.

When I felt as if I needed to improve my communication skills when working with key clients, I looked to a work colleague, Ali Gill, who had a reputation for building solid relationships within the organizations she worked in.

When I started to climb, I quickly found some people who could help guide me to reach my potential, in particular John Dunne and Andy Jack, both superb climbers.

When I sought to increase the amount of charitable work I was doing, I looked for guidance from Dr Adrian Whiteson, one of the founders of the Teenage Cancer Trust.

Who should be your role model?

To help you find your role models, answer these questions:

In what area of your life would you benefit from a role model?

The clearer you are about what area of your life you would like guidance with, the easier it will be to find the right role model for you. To 'be a better manager' might be your overall goal, but try and determine which areas you need to improve on. For example, you might want to improve your ability to give feedback, which in turn will make you a better manager.

Is there someone from within your circle of friends who would be a good role model?

It is estimated that the average person knows 300 people. Take the 300 people you know and multiply them by the 300 people they each know and potentially there's 90,000 people who could be a role model in some area of your life. Obviously you are unlikely to know that many people well enough to decide if they will be suitable as role models. But the chances are, if you need to find someone, for example, who is excellent at giving feedback, then talk to the people you know and they will be able to suggest someone suitable.

Is the person actually the best person for you?

Don't be afraid to move on, and stop using a person as a role model. You may outgrow your role model or realize that they aren't actually the best person for you to model yourself on. If you are simply observing them – are they consistent? If the relationship evolves into that of a mentor – can they communicate in a way that allows you to develop and improve?

ONE STEP BEYOND: MENTORING AND BEING MENTORED

The term 'mentor' comes from Greek mythology. Mentor was

the trusted companion of Odysseus. He assumed the role of advisor, counsellor, tutor and role model to Telemachus, Odysseus's son, when Odysseus set off for the Trojan Wars in circa 800 BC. Today the word 'mentor' has become part of our language, signifying a wise and trusted counsellor and a tutor.

Mentoring is widely recognized as a useful personal development tool in business and general life. In a study of Fortune 500 CEOs, many believed that effective mentoring had played a big part in their success.[1] Women have found mentoring particularly useful as a means of making progress at work. In a survey conducted in 1996, 99% of the female executives interviewed had been mentored.[2]

What can a mentor do for you?

A good mentor can make a big difference to your life. They can help build your confidence, and self worth, and provide you with moral support. They can boost your career, improve skills and help you make professional contacts. They can also provide you with advice, counselling and feedback.

A mentor will take on a variety of roles depending on the kind of relationship (a) you are looking for and (b) they are willing to enter into.

As a counsellor, the mentor can help with personal problems. They can advise on the struggle to maintain a work/life balance and ethical issues such as maintaining personal integrity and values. A good mentor will empathize with you and be able to help you work through and resolve potentially damaging personal internal conflict.

---

[1] Chip R. Bell, *Managers as Mentors: Building Partnerships for Learning*, Berrett-Koehler, 1996.

[2] E. Shaw, 'Mentoring goes modern', *The Arizona Republic*, 7 July 1998.

Another very important role that a mentor can play is as a coach. The advantage of having a coach is well-proven: they keep you motivated when you have trouble motivating yourself, plus they help you to develop skills and techniques to fulfil your goals. They can suggest appropriate strategies for completing tasks as well as providing critical feedback. It's why people have personal trainers, football coaches, CEO coaches and life coaches.

A mentor can act as a supporter. This is particularly useful for very risk-averse people. With the help of supportive mentoring, providing unconditional support and encouragement, you can take more risks and push yourself beyond your normal boundaries. A mentor may also challenge you to better yourself.

Finally, mentors are listeners. Non-judgmental listening is a valuable skill: it requires making a connection. Your mentor may also become your friend, of course.

ROLE MODELS AND MENTORS

I have always had role models, although they tend to be very different people, with very different styles. As a qualified executive coach, I have a supervisor who acts as my own coach.

Most of my role models have been colleagues with whom I have worked and are often in senior positions. I don't think there is such a thing as a perfect leader and I have taken the best from each of those that I have considered to be a mentor. Most of these people have had a profound effect on my working life, my career direction, promotion and so on.

I have a number of close friends who I use as informal mentors with whom I meet frequently and discuss work and life issues.

In turn, I coach and mentor a number of individuals both at work and on a voluntary basis through the Teach First programme.

Richard Cullen
Head of HR, National Probation Service

Where do you find a mentor?

Before looking for a mentor, consider whether you would be suitable for this kind of relationship. Are you an attractive proposition to a mentor? Are you willing to confide in others and willing to learn? If you're not, then why should a mentor give their valuable time to help you?

Mentoring relationships usually have some common characteristics: mentors are usually older than their protégés; it is possible to have more than one mentor at a time; mentoring should benefit both partners equally.

Some organizations run formal mentoring programmes, so you might be able to obtain a mentor this way. Outside of a formal mentoring arrangement, there is informal mentoring. This differs from work mentoring – in informal mentoring, for example, there is no obligation on either party to undertake the relationship in the initial stages. Fans of informal mentoring say that there is a chemistry in the relationships that is lacking in more formal work-mentoring programmes. It is possible to have more than one mentor, covering both work and non-work situations.

How do you actually find your mentor? Quite often, you won't need to; they will find you. Failing this, however, it is up to you to identify and approach potential mentors. You will need to find someone who is a 'good fit'.

There are a number of factors that you should look for when assessing whether the relationship is going to work. Commitment must be a two-way thing; not just the mentor should do the giving. The mentor will want to get something out of the relationship too, so it needs to be mutually rewarding. (Although what is rewarding to the mentor will probably be different from what is rewarding as far as you are concerned.)

Honesty is also essential. You will need to be open and honest with the mentor and share both your successes and failures, otherwise you will be unable to communicate effectively.

Cutting your losses

Not all mentoring relationships work out. Some fail to get off the ground. Some start off OK but grind to a halt. After all, it is difficult to form and maintain relationships in life generally, so why would a mentoring relationship be any different?

You need to be able to spot the signs of an endangered mentoring relationship. Warning signals include:

- your mentor is reluctant to take on difficult issues or participate generally;
- poor communication;
- inappropriate behaviour – the mentor is too bossy or judgemental, or wants an inappropriate relationship; and
- forced participation – good mentoring is unlikely to come from forced participation.

Remember to discuss your plan to get a mentor with your

family or partner. Mentoring relationships can become very close. It is important the boundaries are well managed to avoid them affecting important personal relationships.

ORDINARY PEOPLE, EXTRAORDINARY LIVES

Imagine holding your breath … for three and half minutes. Difficult? Impossible? Now imagine doing it 122 metres under the surface of the ocean. That's what Tanya Streeter does for a living. Born and raised in the Cayman Islands, Streeter is currently the best women's freediver in the world – a sport that involves diving as deep as possible without the use of breathing apparatus.

In 1998, just months after discovering her extraordinary talent for breath-hold diving, Streeter broke both the men's and women's freediving world records. This was in the constant ballast discipline, where she had to descend and ascend completely unassisted. She dived to 185 feet and was underwater for 2 minutes and 10 seconds.

Then, in July 2003, she again broke both the men's and women's world records, this time in the variable weight discipline, where the diver descends on a weighted sled and returns to the surface under his or her own power, either kicking and/or pulling on the rope, or a combination of both. On this occasion, she dived to a depth of 400 feet and was underwater for 3 minutes, 38 seconds.

Equally amazing is the women's world record for static apnea – holding your breath underwater without diving down. The current holder is Lotta Ericson with a staggering 6 minutes, 31 seconds.

WITH A LITTLE HELP

How can we lead our lives in the best possible way? None of us is born with an innate knowledge of how to lead the best life we can live. We all need guidance. How and where we get it is different for each of us. Some find it in religion. For most of us, our parents are role models. Other role models and mentors can be found in the most unexpected places. And all of us have role models; even role models have role models.

The world-famous feminist Germaine Greer, a role model to many women, entertained an audience at All Saints Arts Centre in December 2004. As might be expected, she covered a wide range of subjects and had forthright views on all of them. On the question of role models, she came out against the fictional character Bridget Jones because of the way she makes ineptitude seem a quaint and amusing characteristic for a woman. Instead she preferred as a role model singer and children's author Madonna and news editor and journalist Janet Street-Porter.

NINE

Challenging misconceptions

Prejudice is the reason of fools.
Voltaire

Prejudices, it is well known, are most difficult to eradicate from the heart whose soil has never been loosened or fertilized by education; they grow firm there, firm as weeds among stones.
Charlotte Bronte

THE CHANGING ROOM

As a swimmer you have to lay yourself bare – well, almost. Once you're in your swimwear, there is little left to the imagination, so I very quickly got used to people looking at my artificial leg and, when I took that off, staring at my stump. Children will look straight at me, but adults tend to look out of the corner of their eye and try to hide their thoughts. Just occasionally, they let the mask slip – and you get an insight into how negative impressions of disability pass from generation to generation.

One particular event springs to mind. I was in the changing rooms at the Barnet Copthall swimming pool in North London. There are two swimming pools and a diving pit there, so it is not unusual for members of the swimming team to be getting changed at the same time as the general public.

As I stood there in my swimwear, a young boy of about three noticed me. He was transfixed by the sight of my artificial leg, pointing at it and saying: 'Look, Daddy.'

As soon as his father, who was drying the boy down, realized what his son was pointing at, he slapped him hard across the legs. It took me by surprise. The child wailed and began to cry. I walked out of the changing room, past the sobbing child and flustered parent, not knowing what to say. For the entire training session that followed, I replayed the incident in my head and thought about what I should have said. That child left the pool that day no doubt thinking that disability was a terrible thing, not to be acknowledged or talked about.

What's on the label?

We all use labels. 'Fat', 'stupid', 'disabled', 'artistic', 'practical', 'academic' – the list is endless. Businesses would be lost without them.

Marketers categorize us in many different ways. There are socio-economic classes. The most recent government classification by the Office for National Statistics classifies us all as one of the following:

- higher managerial and professional occupations;
- large employers and higher managerial occupations;
- higher professional occupations;
- lower managerial and professional occupations;
- intermediate occupations;
- small employers and own account workers;
- lower supervisory and technical occupations;
- semi-routine occupations;
- routine occupations; and
- never worked and long-term unemployed.

Then there are generational labels: baby boomers, Generation X, Generation E, Generation Y. Not forgetting all those acronyms: YUPPIES (young urban professionals), DINKS (double income, no kids). Without labels, the media would suffer too. A stock favourite in magazines is an article that categorizes readers according to their clothes, eating habits, taste in music or sexual peccadilloes.

Labelling becomes subconscious. How many times do you meet someone and, because they remind you of someone you have met before, you put them in the same category?

We use labels for several reasons. For a start, people are complicated. Complicated is messy – it is much easier to make sense of the world if we categorize and pigeonhole people. Think of a few people you know – how do you define them? Probably with just a few words, such as 'neat', 'bad-tempered' or 'ambitious'.

Categorizing like this is normal human activity. Research has shown that children can distinguish between social groups at a very early age, and categorize between genders in the first year of life.[1]

'The human mind must think with the aid of categories ... Once formed, categories are the basis for normal prejudgement. We cannot possibly avoid this process. Orderly living depends upon it,' said US psychologist Gordon Allport in his book *The Nature of Prejudice*.[2]

The problem is that we cheat others and we cheat ourselves by using labels. We don't bother to find out what people are really like. Labels are deceptive; they generalize – stereotype, in other words. They tell us nothing about the individual. They feed prejudice and discrimination.

prejudice noun; an unfair and unreasonable opinion or feeling, especially when formed without enough thought or knowledge.

Why labels matter

Labels and prejudice go hand in hand. When we categorize people, we tend to do so in terms of 'us and them', or what the scientists call ingroups and outgroups. We favour members of the ingroup that we feel a part of. We exaggerate the similarities between members of the same category and the differences between members of different categories: the perceived

---

[1] J.A. Cameron, J.M. Alvarez, D.N. Ruble and A.J. Fuligni, 'Children's lay theories about ingroups and outgroups: reconceptualizing research on "prejudice"', *Personality and Social Psychology Review* 5:118–28, 2001.
[2] Gordon Allport, *The Nature of Prejudice*, Addison-Wesley, 1954.

wisdom that all disabled people are the same as each other and completely different from able-bodied people, for example.

Even apparently arbitrary connections can exert a powerful influence over us. We are more likely to co-operate with someone if we discover that they share the same birthday.[3] And women are more likely to marry men whose surname starts with the same letter as their own.[4]

Don't think that labelling is innocuous or harmless. What starts as a convenient way to categorize people can become something far more sinister. Here's a list of coloured shapes: blue triangle, brown triangle, red triangle, green triangle, yellow star, pink triangle. Some of you may recognize them. They are labels – badges sewn onto clothes. Labels that signified whether the wearer was a foreign forced labourer, a political prisoner, a Romany, a criminal, Jewish or gay. Labels that invariably meant incarceration, and probably death, in a Nazi concentration camp.

The use of standard labels and phrases can further feed negativity. When I was first diagnosed with cancer and as I started my treatment, some people would refer to me as a 'cancer sufferer' or a 'cancer victim'. I despised these phrases. They were so negative and I just wanted to hold onto a positive outlook.

At the time the cancer wasn't making me suffer. It was the chemotherapy that was making me suffer, but have you ever heard of anyone being referred to as a 'chemotherapy

---

[3] D.T. Miller, J. Downs and D.A. Prentice, 'Minimal conditions for the creation of an unit relationship: the social bond between birthdaymates', *European Journal of Social Psychology* 28:475–81, 1998.

[4] J.T. Jones, B.W. Pelham, M. Carvallo and M.C. Mirenberg, 'How do I love thee? Let me count the Js: implicit egotism and interpersonal attraction', *Journal of Personality and Social Psychology* 87:665–83, 2004.

sufferer'? As for being called a cancer victim … I didn't want to be a victim, I wanted to be a survivor. Why were people talking about me as if I was already dead?

EXPERIENCING PREJUDICE

I tendered for a job many years ago for a high-profile band. I went for a meeting with the managing director of the record label and as soon as I walked in, I knew that I didn't have the job because I was Asian and too young. The guy practically told me as much and I left in disgust. Since then I vowed never to be intimidated by old-school bullshit attitudes again. My determination, drive and ambitious ideas just needed to wait for the right opportunity.

Kumar Kamalagharan
Managing Director, Fruit Pie Music

Sticky labels

Once established, both stereotypes and prejudice can be incredibly hard to overcome. They can affect careers, relationships, and every aspect of someone's life.

A good example of how stereotypes stick and become entrenched comes from an experiment in which participants were asked to judge the heights of men and women from photos. Each photo was of a man or woman. The participants were told that for each picture of a man in the group of photos, there was also one of a woman of equal height. They were also told that they should judge each photo as an individual case, and not to rely on a person's sex when judging. Even though there was a cash prize available for the most accurate judge, the participants were still unable to disregard the stereotyped categories of male and female and judged males a few inches taller than the female on average.[5]

It happens outside of the research lab too, in the real world. Even though when people talk about prejudice and discrimination, most of us think of racism, sexism and other more obvious forms of prejudice, stereotyping comes in all shapes and sizes. Even in apparently harmless forms.

A friend of mine was labelled an 'academic' by his parents. This was because he excelled at school. Whenever he attempted to do anything practical, his parents would laugh and tell him not to bother. He subsequently became a proficient musician, laid concrete foundations, built a garden shed and dismantled and rebuilt various pieces of electronic equipment. In fact, he could do most things he turned his hand to. His friends know this. The rest of his family still think of him as 'academic' and think that he is hopeless at anything practical.

ARE YOU PREJUDICED?

Ask yourself the following questions to see if your own prejudices are clouding your judgements and potentially holding you back:

---

[5] T.E. Nelson, M.R. Biernat and M. Manis, 'Everyday base rates (sex stereotypes): potent and resilient', *Journal of Personality and Social Psychology* 59:664–75, 1990.

- Are you basing your opinion on stereotypical information or specifically on the individual?
- Are you letting your past experience of another individual with similar characteristics affect your judgement?
- Do you make your own mind up or are you being swayed by the opinions of others?
- Are you focusing on obstacles or attributes?
- Do you instantly criticise or do you put yourself in their shoes and empathize?

WITHOUT PREJUDICE

Labels, prejudice, discrimination – it may all seem academic unless you are a victim. Most of us, at some time or another, have been a victim of prejudice. Have you ever been dismissed as stupid, ugly, bright, beautiful, fat, thin, lazy, hard-working? And there are many other categories. Most of us too have at some time or another been guilty of stereotyping and being prejudiced. Have *you* ever dismissed someone else as stupid, ugly, bright, beautiful, fat, thin, lazy, hard-working? Or one of many other categories?

But this is a self-help book, so why should we care? How are labels, stereotyping, prejudice and discrimination related to being the best person we can be? Well, for a start, victims can be prevented from achieving their personal best. If someone stops me from getting a promotion, or being on a sports team because of stereotyping and prejudice about my disability, then they are an obstacle to my personal development.

Stereotyping also has a more subtle effect on the way I perform. Studies have shown that when college students are shown stereotypical words and pictures relating to old age, they walk more slowly and perform less well in word recognition tests. Other students 'primed' with football hooligan stereotypes performed less well in general knowledge tests versus students primed with professor stereotyping.[6] Women taking a difficult maths test wearing a swimsuit – 'bimbo' – performed less well than when wearing normal daywear. Men showed no difference in performance.[7]

The motivation for removing stereotyping and prejudice is clear for the victims, but what about the perpetrators? When we label others, when we are prejudiced against others without good reason, we close off part of the world. We narrow our world view. Life is a team event. We are social creatures. You can never be your very best entirely through your own endeavours. Approach the world with a bunch of prejudices and your team is likely to be a lot smaller than it could or should be.

And, equally important, this chapter is here because I strongly believe the world would be a better place without prejudice. Sure there may be times when it is useful. As a soldier fighting a war for example, it may pay to be prejudiced against the enemy. But for the most part prejudice is harmful to society. I have experienced it at first hand, both in relation to cancer and to disability. Believe me when I tell you, we are a better society without it. And you will be a better person without it.

---

[6] K. Kawakami, H. Young and J.F. Dovidio, 'Automatic stereotyping: category, trait, and behavioral activations', *Personality and Social Psychology Bulletin* 28:3–15, 2002.

[7] B.L. Fredrickson, T.A. Roberts, S.M. Noll, D.M. Quinn and J.M. Twenge, 'That swimsuit becomes you: sex differences in self-objectification, restrained eating and math performance', *Journal of Personality and Social Psychology* 75:269–84, 1998.

DEALING WITH PREJUDICE

Unfortunately there is no magic potion that you can take that will rid you of prejudice. And, as you have learnt, stereotypes and prejudice can be deep seated and hard to shift. However, there are some things you can do that will help.

Communicate and connect

Confront stereotypes. Don't avoid contact and communication. A classic example is the 'Does he take sugar?' syndrome – addressing comments to an able-bodied person accompanying a disabled person, rather than to the disabled person directly.

Does he take sugar? by Michael W. Williams[8]

'Does he take sugar in his tea?'
Hello; why not ask me?
I might have a disability,
But to answer for myself I still have the ability.
Just 'cos I'm not stood up like you:
Does not mean there is very little for myself that I can do.
Some people think we're sick
And others a little bit thick.
Well, how many O Levels have you got?
As many as me, I'll bet not!
I also have a university honours degree!
A brainy sod that's me.

---

[8] Taken from *Weirs of Tears and Miles of Smiles – Simple Poetry from the Heart*. Reproduced by permission of Michael W. Williams

To my mum people will say: Is this your son?
Tell me, how's he getting on?
Mum's reply is: Well he's certainly not dim,
So why don't you ask him?

As it happens, I do take sugar. And while I have yet to suffer the indignity of the sugar question, I have certainly encountered prejudice as a barrier to communication. People have labelled me as disabled and consequently treated me differently.

I have had it happen to me where someone has talked over the top of me, about me, whilst I was putting on my artificial leg. A senior official at the 2004 swimming Olympic trials came up to me and then turned slightly to ask the person next to me, 'Is he ready to go to his presentation?' The other person looked at me dumbfounded. I wanted to say something along the lines of 'To my knowledge, having an artificial leg does not affect my eyesight, hearing or intellectual ability.' But I simply stood up, looked down at him and said: 'Yes, I'm ready.'

It is not just in the case of disability where this happens. Women often have to work a lot harder to make themselves visible. A female friend of mine had builders in to do some work. The problem was the builders only wanted to talk to her husband. Every time she tried to explain something to them they called her 'love' or 'duck' and treated her like an idiot, even though she was a very well-educated woman. Needless to say they didn't refer to her husband as 'love', 'duck' or any other term of endearment – just 'Mr'.

How many times do a man and a woman go into a store together, and the salesperson direct their comments to the man?

Make sure you don't behave this way.

Empathize – put yourself in the shoes of others

In the 1400s, the Catholic Church was effectively at war with non-Christians. As a result, a number of papal bulls (sealed decrees by letter from the Pope) were issued – the *Dum Diversas* in 1452 and the *Romanus Pontifex* in 1455, for example – granting various kings the rights to territory they might discover, provided it wasn't already owned by Christians. This doctrine of discovery was further enshrined in papal law following Columbus's journey to Hispaniola – modern-day Haiti and the Dominican Republic. The doctrine of discovery was effectively the legal foundation upon which European powers seized land in the Americas.

In September 1973, Native Indian activist Adam Fortunate Eagle was invited to be a delegate at an international conference in Rome. When he arrived at Leonardo Da Vinci Airport, he was greeted by a throng of reporters. Stepping onto the runway in full tribal outfit, Fortunate Eagle announced: 'In the name of the American Indian people, and pursuant of the Doctrine of Discovery, I hereby lay claim to this land called Italy.' By what authority did Fortunate Eagle lay claim to Italy? As Fortunate Eagle noted: 'What right did Columbus have to discover America when it had already been inhabited for thousands of years? The same right I now have to come to Italy and proclaim the discovery of your country.'[9]

When you adopt a different perspective – put yourself in the shoes of Fortunate Eagle – it becomes easier to understand why the Native Indians might feel aggrieved over claims that

---

[9] www.chronogram.com/issue/2001/06/conversation.htm, *Miami News*, 23 September 1973.

Columbus 'discovered' America, or the celebration of Columbus Day.

As children, we have all pretended to be something else: slid across the floor pretending to be a snake; rolled into a ball; stood up tall with our arms out like a tree. Now close your eyes and imagine the complexities of being disabled, black or Muslim in a Westernized country. Imagine what things would impact on your life. Appreciate the differences. Then recognize the similarities – the fact that the person you are imagining is also *the same* as you. They are a person with hopes and fears, capable of good and bad, success and failure – trying to live their life.

If you can do this, then you are on the way to being empathetic.

ORDINARY PEOPLE, EXTRAORDINARY LIVES

Growing up in north-east Scotland, Evelyn Glennie was keen on music. She played the clarinet and the harmonica. Aged eight, however any musical aspirations seemed impossible when she developed problems with her hearing. By the age of 12, she was profoundly deaf. Undaunted, Glennie swapped instruments. She switched to the snare drum, attuned her body to be sensitive to vibration and differences in pitch depending on how she perceived the vibration, and determined to become a professional percussionist.

Today Glennie is one of the world's leading percussionists, and the first to make a living as a solo percussionist. She performs over a hundred concerts a year and has won countless awards, including a BAFTA and a Grammy, and has been awarded an the OBE for her services to music.

Learn to love yourself

Stereotyping not only allows us to categorize others but it helps us affirm our own identity. Just as we label others, we label ourselves. We use identification with a group to boost our self-esteem. Research has shown that people suffering a drop in self-esteem are more likely to show prejudice.

If prejudice and stereotyping are ways of boosting self-esteem, equally, by boosting self-esteem it is possible to reduce prejudice. It may sound unlikely, but merely by focusing on the things that you are good at and that help you feel good about yourself, you may reduce your tendency to be prejudiced.

Help yourself

So far I have outlined action that we can take to avoid stereotyping and being prejudiced towards others. But there is also action that the victims of prejudice can take. If you are a victim, you might ask: 'Why should I bother if I'm not the person at fault?' It's a fair question, but if you are waiting for other people to change their attitudes, you could be waiting for some time. Surely it is better to help yourself if you can.

In the essay 'Motivating individuals to change: what is a target to do?', Stanford University psychology professor Jennifer Eberhardt and Princeton psychology professor Susan Fiske outline a variety of strategies to minimize stereotyping.[9] These include:

---

[9] J.L. Eberhardt and S.T. Fiske, 'Motivating individuals to change: what is a target to do?' In: C.N. Macrae, C. Stangor and M. Hewstone (eds.), *Stereotypes and Stereotyping*, Guilford Press, 1996.

- Stress areas of similarity with majority group members. This encourages them not to view you as a member of a stereotyped outgroup.
- Whenever possible, make it quite clear what your values are, for example in terms of fairness, equality and so on. This will encourage the group to follow those values. Also, reinforce those values by praising and rewarding those who demonstrate them.
- Because people naturally like to categorize, try to get people to categorize you in a way you want to be perceived. Do this by reinforcing their views of you. The more you demonstrate to people how smart you are, and tell them so, the more likely they are to perceive you as such.
- Keep clear of those people most likely to act in a prejudiced way, such as people who have suffered a loss of self-esteem or who are insecure. Also, remember that in the same way that you can avoid being prejudiced against them by seeing the world through their eyes, you should remember that they may see you differently. Often behaviour can be interpreted in many different ways – all of them correct, depending on the perspective.

We have to be aware that different people will perceive the same attributes and responses completely differently. A tall blonde female walking alone along the streets of Stockholm will not get a second glance. However, if the same woman were to walk along the streets of Jeddah, the reactions of the people will be totally different.

I am of course used to people glancing at my artificial leg as I walk down the street in a pair of shorts. However, I was taken aback by the reaction that people had when I visited Singapore on a training camp. People would cross the road to take a better look at my artificial leg. One man came up to me as I waited for the MRT (Singapore's subway system), crouched down right next to me and began to examine my artificial leg. Not once did he look me in the eye. It wasn't until afterwards, when it was explained to me that disabled people are often hidden away in Singapore, that I began to understand his actions – even though I didn't feel comfortable with them.

Our actions as individuals can be viewed very differently. When looking at my life in general, someone might consider me to be very focused and determined. Someone else may think that I am selfish and arrogant. My actions are the same just perceived differently. I have to accept both of those points of view because everyone has the right to their own opinion (provided they are not breaking the law). Whether I agree or disagree with them. I just have to live my life the best that I can and make the appropriate decisions to do that.

A WOMAN IN A MAN'S WORLD

My job title is 'painter and decorator', which is a blanket description and covers a multitude of skills. I do predominantly decorate but I can also tile, build shelving, do electrical work, lay flooring, mix cement and pretty much do anything to do with the home.

Every day that I work I face some form of prejudice and levels of sexism that are dictated by the amount of men I am working with.

To put this into perspective for you, imagine a building site where there are ten men standing around cracking jokes, telling stories and for the most part chatting in a generally derogatory way about women. In I walk and the men are already threatened, just because I have a different chromosome to them and they can see that I am dressed in paint-covered working clothes. Already I am facing a form of prejudice and I haven't even picked up a paintbrush yet. The expectations on me are far greater than if another man walked in to that situation – I have to prove myself as a woman and as a worker, and I do that every day by doing what I do best. I let my work do the talking for me, and who can argue with that?

Petra Markell
Interior designer

Look at the world differently

As part of my charitable work, I visit schools. I believe it is imperative that children are educated about prejudiced attitudes towards others. I talk about subjects ranging from cancer to sport, from disability to relationships with friends. In the year before finishing this book, I spoke to approximately 50,000 schoolchildren. Changing the misconceptions of society is something we can all help with. I'm not arrogant enough to think that I can do it on my own, but if I can improve the way just one child looks at the world, then it is worth the effort.

At schools, children ask me how I cope with being disabled. I try to challenge their way of thinking:

'Let me ask you a question. Who is the most disabled person in this room?'

'You are,' they say. 'You only have one leg.'

'OK. Who is the fastest swimmer in this room?'

'You are,' they say. 'You have a gold medal.'

'Right. So who is disabled at swimming, you or me?'

At this point, you can see them trying to come to terms with the fact that they might be disabled. The point that I try to make to them is that disability is relative to the task at hand.

Take any individual and they will have a range of abilities, depending on the task at hand. On the ability scale I am towards the 'able' end for swimming. When it comes to spelling, however, I am towards the 'unable' or 'disabled' end. Just because your disability inhibits you from doing certain things well, it doesn't mean that you can't do other things exceptionally.

Occasionally I will receive something from a child who understands the point I am trying to make. The piece below was given to me by a tiny slip of a girl at a school in Middlesbrough.

One bright sunny day, Kimberley woke up. Kimberley couldn't walk. Kimberley was a child. Her father helped her with everything. When she woke up, she stretched out and called her Dad with a little buzzer that she and her Dad had on their beds. Her Dad came in and got her clothes. He said, 'We're going to the swimming baths.'

Kimberley had moved from Middlesbrough to Eston.

'Whooppee!'

Her Dad helped her dress and get in the wheelchair. They had breakfast. Kimberley had never been to Eston Swimming Baths before.

They got changed and went in. They heard someone say, 'Hey! You! Wheely! Ha, ha, ha! You can't walk! Ha ha!'

Kimberley started to cry, but her Dad said, 'Don't you worry, just come in the baths and you'll forget about it.'

Although Kimberley could not walk, she was a very good swimmer. In fact, when she got out, the boy that had called her names had been watching and when Kimberley looked at him, he was sitting there. His face was blank like a fish. He was opening and shutting his mouth as if he wanted to say something. Kimberley giggled at him.

'Ha ha, now who's the silly one?'

The boy couldn't say anything. He just stared. Kimberley and her Dad went home and she, whenever she went to Eston Swimming Baths, was never called any names again.

Jessica Dennison (8 years old)
Pallister Park Primary School

Children sometimes grasp the point much more easily than an adult.

TEN

What does success look like?

You have power over your mind – not outside events.
Realize this, and you will find strength.
Marcus Aurelius

A man is but the product of his thoughts.
What he thinks he becomes.
Mahatma Gandhi

A SLICE OF LUCK

When judging the quality of an Olympic village the primary considerations for an athlete are:

* Can I get a good night's sleep?
* Can I get the right types of food at times that suit me?
* Is the journey to the competition venue going to be easy and hassle-free?

If these three requirements are met, athletes usually turn their attention to the social facilities. Although these help the athletes pass time while waiting to compete, they are used much more enthusiastically once the athlete's competition schedule is over.

The Olympic village in Barcelona was fantastic in all respects.

The accommodation was comfortable, the substantial dining room catered for every taste and was open 24/7, and the transport system was ultra-efficient. However, it was because of Barcelona's ability to deliver that little bit extra that many experienced athletes still consider it the best Olympic village ever.

There was plenty to keep restless athletes occupied: a cinema, cafés, a games room including 200 metres of Scalextric track and a ten-pin bowling centre, for a start. But for most, the highlight was the fact that it had its own stretch of private beach.

My Barcelona Paralympics had finished after the 100m backstroke. So one morning, after my room-mate Paul Noble had left to compete in the heats of the 200 individual medley, I grabbed my sun protection and wandered down to the beach to reflect on the Games and contemplate my future swimming career. It was a glorious summer's day and I spent a leisurely couple of hours listening to the waves and watching people admire the huge metal fish sculpture by Frank O. Gehry before eventually heading for the food hall and, finally, back to the room.

When I got back to the twin room, I couldn't believe the scene in front of me. The room had been ransacked. All the drawers were emptied onto the floor and the contents of the wardrobes had been pulled out. Paul was sorting through the mess on the floor.

'What the hell's happened?' I asked, thinking we had been robbed.

'I've lost it!' Paul said. From the frantic tone in his voice it seemed that he had. Completely.

'What have you lost?'

'My pizza bag.'

'Your *what?*'

'My lucky pizza bag!'

Paul then recounted the story of his lucky pizza bag. A few years before, he ordered a takeaway pizza that was delivered in a plastic bag. The next day, he used the bag to take some of his swimming kit to a competition and put in one of his best swimming performances ever. Ever since then, he took the bag to every race he swam in. He had qualified for the final that evening but couldn't find the lucky pizza bag.

I looked at him, and then down at the bag that I had used to carry my sun cream to the beach. On the side it said 'Express Pizza'. Oops.

'Would this be it, by any chance?'

Fortunately, Paul was more relieved to see the bag than he was cross with me. It took him a while to calm down but he managed to eventually. That evening he swam the race of his life, winning the gold medal by just three one-hundredths of a second.

Now who can say whether the pizza bag helped Paul to win his gold? Personally I suspect his victory had more to do with the hard training he did in preparation for the Paralympics. Did it provide him with that little extra confidence? And if he had lost his pizza bag altogether, would his frame of mind have been so badly affected that he would have lost the race?

A LITTLE SOMETHING EXTRA?

The things I have already written about – goal setting, teamwork, motivation, communication, a desire to be the best you can possibly be – will get you long way. They will get you further than you might have imagined was possible. Further than you realized you were capable of. But there is always room for improvement – always a little bit extra available.

Anyone with a perfectionist streak will recognize the need to go that extra mile, or inch, to achieve that little bit more. In professional sports it is often the difference between a good performance and a personal best performance. At work, it might mean you giving a great presentation rather than an OK one, or getting a second interview rather than a rejection letter.

What is it, then, that adds that little bit extra, that gives your performance a slight edge? It may be something physiological that affects your physical state for the better. Or it may be something psychological that gives you a mental edge. Even something that does both.

There will always be some people who resort to illegal means. Will anyone who saw it forget the sight of Ben Johnson running the 100m at the Seoul Olympics in 1988 in a world record time of 9.79 seconds? Shortly after, however, Johnson tested positive for the anabolic steroid stanozolol and was eventually stripped of his gold medal.

But there are non-pharmacological ways to get an edge. Their advantage is that they are not illegal or damaging to your health. There are many techniques that you can use, either on your own or with the assistance of someone else. Admittedly, some may sound a little crazy, but it's really a question of 'don't knock it unless you've tried it'. If it is not harmful or illegal, it can't hurt to try. If it doesn't work for you, you've lost nothing but a little time and effort. If it helps you improve your life, then it was worth it.

PICTURING SUCCESS

I use a simple visualization technique during important business meetings or presentations, and encourage my staff to do the same.

Think of something which you feel comfortable and confident performing: a sport, a language – anything. For me, I imagine myself on a rather ridiculous piece of gym equipment called a Versaclimber. For some strange reason I am able to 'climb' for a mile on this contraption in a very respectable time. Although no match for any serious athlete, I have always posted the best score in every gym I have been to.

Just before my meetings, I imagine myself going head-to-head with the person I am meeting on the Versaclimber. I know I will beat him, and if not it will be close enough not to matter. This allows me to believe that we are equal adversaries. He may have a tough reputation, but I know he's going to suffer just like me with 200 metres to go on that climb! You'd be surprised how effective this is and how varied the activities are that other people choose to visualize, ranging from cooking Pavlova to speaking Urdu.

Richard Davies
CEO, ATP Properties

GETTING IT RIGHT ON THE NIGHT

So what are these techniques that can help squeeze a little extra performance out, help you get through the day in one rather than several pieces?

They range from the commonsense to the slightly left-field. The use of lucky charms is a good example. It worked for Paul in his swimming and it works for many others. Relaxation routines can put you in the performing frame of mind. Self-talk can remove doubts and worries. Hypnosis can help overcome a fear or remove a craving. Visualization helps you see success. Pre-performance rituals can prepare you for action.

So here are a just few. It's not a comprehensive list and I haven't tried them all – although in each case, I know someone who has. They may work for you; the only way to find out is by trying.

- self-talk and affirmation;
- the 'fiction into fact' technique;
- visualization;
- hypnosis;

- practice; and
- relaxation techniques.

Self-talk and affirmation

Self-talk and affirmations are two techniques that can help you to overcome self-doubt, stay calm under pressure and improve performance. Affirmations are strong positive statements that, when read or spoken aloud, boost an individual's self-esteem. They can help to reduce your heart rate and blood pressure.

One of the best examples of how effective affirmation can be is the boxer Muhammad Ali. His battle cry 'I am the greatest!' was known across the world long before he was considered the finest boxer of all time. Self-talk is the same process but conducted as a private inner dialogue. We all carry on an internal dialogue from time to time – the more positive it is, the more our self-esteem and self-belief will be improved.

The key is keeping self-talk and affirmations positive. Negative self-talk, for example, is more likely to lead to failure than success. Telling yourself you are useless, that you can't do it or, that you are stupid, eats into your self-esteem and is likely to become a self-fulfilling prophesy. (Equally, telling others the same thing will lower their self-esteem.)

Instead, nurture a sense of self-belief and self-esteem. Talk positively to yourself and others. Believe in yourself. If you are about to go for an interview, tell yourself that you are an excellent candidate, you have the necessary skills and knowledge, and will be an asset to your potential employers.

In team situations, boost the self-esteem of your teammates. People with low self-esteem typically focus on trying to prove themselves or impress others. They often act with arrogance and contempt towards others, focusing on their own personal gain, and when things don't go right they are quick to blame others rather than take responsibility for their actions. Team members with high self-esteem and a positive outlook are more likely to be constructive, responsible and trustworthy.

Self-talk and affirmations are both techniques that I have used to good effect. Recently I was attempting a difficult climb that had previously defeated me. Approximately two-thirds of the way up I reached the point where I'd fallen off before. My toes were on a couple of tiny footholds and my left hand on an awkward hold. I needed to make my self safe and, with my right hand, clip the rope into a metal clip that was already attached to the rock face. As I took hold of the rope, I repeated to myself: 'You can do it, you can do it, you can do it.' It helped me focus and stay calm, and this time I completed the climb.

The 'fiction into fact' technique

Closely related to the idea of self-talk and affirmation, this is based on the idea that if you say or do something for long enough, it will eventually happen. In Greek mythology, Pygmalion believed so strongly that his ivory statue of a woman was real, the goddess Venus gave it life.

So, for example, if you practise smiling over an extended period, then eventually you will smile without realizing it, and hopefully feel happy into the bargain. Interestingly, smiling seems to be infectious – see *Happy, smiling people*, below. If you smile, other people smile, although if you are going to try this be careful where.

HAPPY, SMILING PEOPLE

The subject of emotions is a hotly debated one among psychologists. What causes emotion? One theory, suggested independently by US psychologist William James and Danish physiologist Carl Lange in 1884, is that the signs of emotions – smiling, frowning, crying – are not the *product* of emotion but the *cause* of them. So smiling causes happiness and crying causes sadness.

If the 'facial feedback' hypothesis is true, then the more we smile, the better we feel. In one study, participants watched cartoons while holding a pencil either between their lips or teeth. Those who held the pencil between the lips – and were thus prevented from smiling – didn't think the cartoons were as funny as those holding a pencil with their teeth and who were able to smile.[1]

This is not a technique I use. Muhammad Ali presumably did. He once said about his repeated exclamations of being the greatest: 'I figured if I said it enough, I would convince the world that I really was the greatest.'

Personally, I think whilst it is useful to have a positive mental attitude, there has to be some grounding in reality. Do I believe that if I say I'm going to win the lottery enough times it will happen? No.

On the other hand, if I tell everybody how bright I am, often enough, maybe they'll believe me – even if it is not true. So I can see how this might be useful in terms of influencing

---

[1] S.F. Davis and J.J. Palladino, J. J., *Psychology* (third edition), Prentice-Hall, 2000.

the way people perceive you, which in turn reinforces the way you feel. And indeed several people have told me that it does work this way. After all, there are enough leaders out there who became leaders by telling everybody they are leaders.

Visualization

As I open my eyes I sense a chill in the air – the air conditioning unit in my bedroom is keeping the mid-afternoon Alabama heat at bay. After cleaning my teeth and putting on a tracksuit, I pick up my kit bag, repacked after my swim in the heats, and walk up the hill to the swimming pool, collecting a bottle of my favourite blue Powerade drink along the way.

I go through a preset warm-up routine and then make my way to the call-up room. All the usual suspects from previous encounters at World and European championships are there, plus a couple of new faces. As we march onto the poolside the crowd roars.

I can feel the harsh surface of the starting block under my foot as I step up onto it. The crowd falls silent, the electronic bleep goes and the race begins. A couple of technical checks of my stroke and each one is perfect as I control my power down the first length and then back towards the finish, having executed an excellent turn. I touch the wall, see that I have won and punch the air.

Then I drift off to a well-earned sleep, tucked under my duvet, my alarm already set for morning training at my local swimming pool.

Each night, in the year that preceded the Atlanta Paralympics, I lay in bed before I went to sleep and visualized the races I was going to compete in. I went through every detail. How I would feel as I walked onto the poolside. What I would be thinking as I prepared for the start. The sensation of the starting block underfoot. The start, the finish and every stroke in between.

It is incredible how visualizing a potentially intense experience on a regular basis can help you mentally prepare for the moment you have to perform for real. When I touched the starting block for the first time, a week before my first race, I felt as if I had been there hundreds of times before. It allowed me to focus on the task and not be distracted by everything going on around me. I wasn't even aware of the thousands of spectators watching poolside or the millions watching on TV.

This kind of visualization is a technique commonly employed by sportsmen and women, and involves the mental enactment of the task about to be undertaken with a successful outcome attached. It is a great way of acclimatizing to a difficult task. Sir Edmund Hilary, for example, climbed Mount Everest many times in his mind before he scaled the peak for real. Use this technique to walk through whatever it is you want to do well. Imagine every aspect of what you will be doing, all the senses, and how you feel and think, and of course imagine a positive outcome.

VISUALIZATION

I would use visual tools to help with motivation. Sometimes more advanced techniques such as visualization were too tiring at that point. The night before the race, I would look through photos of me swimming – and particularly winning! – to remember how great it felt to swim fast. Before the race itself I would look at flash cards with motivating words and phrases.

Georgina Lee
British Olympian

Hypnosis

How often have you seen an advertisement that says 'Lose weight and quit smoking. The power of hypnosis'? Hypnosis is an increasingly popular means of breaking a habit or strengthening a belief. It works by relaxing and focusing an individual in such a way as to create a state of what has become known as hyper-suggestibility. I have friends who have tried and failed to give up smoking using a variety of methods, and have stopped after just one hypnosis session.

Another GB Paralympic swim team member, Giles Long, used hypnosis to help him get into mental shape to win gold. He decided to use hypnosis because he felt he was becoming scared of driving himself to his maximum. Any kind of exertion at your physical limit is very painful and after years on the swimming circuit, with the regular grind of training and competition, he felt he had become jaded and had created a mental barrier between swimming at 99.5% and 100%. Although he was in great shape physically it wasn't worth leaving anything to chance going into Paralympic year.

Giles saw a professional hypnotist who used hypnosis to embed a trigger phrase into his subconscious, so that when he used that particular phrase he felt physically refreshed. The phrase was 'Increase the power!' and he used it in the final 20 metres of the 100m butterfly in Sydney. Giles said it gave him renewed control, sharpness and strength for the closing stages of the race. He returned home with the gold medal.

Pre-performance rituals

Many of the world's greatest performers, whether it is in the sports or the arts, have set pre-performance rituals. It might be just a huddle before going out on stage, or it might be a detailed schedule of what kit to put on first, what food to eat and in what order, or whether to be the first or last team member out of the changing room.

The rugby player Jonny Wilkinson has a pre-match routine that involves a shave, a shower and then listening to a mental rehearsal CD. It also incorporates both affirmation and visualization techniques. Other successful sports athletes are no different. Famous US baseball player Wade Boggs used to eat fried chicken at 2pm exactly before every game; basketball superstar Michael Jordan used to wear a 'lucky' pair of shorts underneath his Chicago Bulls outfit.

The best-known examples may be from the world of sport, but the idea of preparing yourself physically and mentally for action in this way is not confined to sporting superstars. We can all benefit from a pre-performance routine, especially before an activity we do a lot.

One time I was in Sheffield shopping with my mum shortly before attending a hospital appointment. It was when I was just starting out on my series of chemo treatments. There is a lot of hanging around when your life becomes entangled with the NHS, so Mum and I often found ourselves browsing the shops of Sheffield before I attended a hospital appointment there.

On one such shopping excursion, Mum bought me a T-shirt. On the front there was a picture of a tennis player desperately diving to make a shot and below the image was the score.

I wore the T-shirt when I went in for my next treatment. Dr Willis, one of the team of oncologists looking after me, came into my room.

'Let's have a look at that T-shirt, Marc,' he said. So I sat up straight and showed him.

'Excellent,' he said. 'A fighting back T-shirt.'

I looked down again at the man striving to win and took a closer look at the sequence of scores written beneath him. 40–0, 40–15, 40–30, deuce.

Inside I knew I was fighting already, but this comment made the fight more real and created a ritual at the same time. The shirt became a symbol of my fight and I always pulled it on as I faced my chemotherapy.

Rituals really can create a winning state of mind. They can be the start of a well-trodden path that leads to success. Remember, though, if you choose to do this, or find yourself doing it, only create rituals that can *always* be completed. Otherwise, if you are unable to complete the ritual, doubt will creep in and have a negative effect on your performance.

Also, be careful not to let a pre-performance ritual assume too great an importance. Obsessive compulsive disorder (OCD) may be a familiar term to many of you. Have you ever gone back to check the gas or electricity is turned off before going on holiday, or avoided touching taps or door handles in a public toilet because of germs, or felt the need to lay things in straight lines or other patterns or do things in a certain order? Multiply this to the nth degree and you have OCD. For sufferers it can make their lives unliveable. So don't let the rituals take over your life.

ORDINARY PEOPLE, EXTRAORDINARY LIVES

To most the challenge of climbing Mount Everest is the challenge of a lifetime. Few of us will stand on top of the world. Those that are lucky enough to attempt it, succeed and live to tell the tale will know how tough a proposition climbing the world's highest mountain is.

Winds gust at more than 125mph and the air is thin – there is only a third of the oxygen available at sea level. Even with the benefit of bottled oxygen, likely medical complications include frostbite, hypothermia, pulmonary oedema (where the lungs fill with liquid and you drown) and cerebral oedema (where your brain swells up). Not to mention other complications such as falling off of the mountain or down a crevasse, or being buried beneath an avalanche.

Incredibly, the brilliant Austrian climber Reinhold Messner has climbed Everest twice. Not such a remarkable feat in itself – over 1000 people have now summited – but the first time he climbed it was without bottled oxygen, and the second time he climbed solo without oxygen. Both were firsts. In addition, he was the first person to climb all of the 14 mountain peaks in the world that stand at over 8000 metres.

Practice

OK, so it isn't a technique as such, but it is important to adopt the right attitude to practice.

When it comes to practice, the usual platitude trotted out by parents, teachers and coaches is that 'practice makes perfect'. Broadly speaking this is true, but there is an assumption that you are practising correctly. Incorrect, inaccurate and generally sloppy practice will not make perfect, or anything like perfect. If that is how you practise, then that is how you are likely to perform under pressure. So a better saying is: 'perfect practice makes perfect.'

Watching some video footage of one of my races in 1996, my coach and I realized I needed to improve the way that I turned. I needed to be closer to the wall, rotating in a tighter, faster tuck. Every day in practice I tried to concentrate on this. If I executed a poor turn, I immediately stopped what I was doing and returned to do the turn again, but this time perfectly.

It was this attitude to training and preparation that helped me, at the age of 35, achieve a lifetime personal best just six weeks before my professional swimming career came to end.

Relaxation techniques

Often simply having a more relaxed frame of mind and physiology can have a positive impact on your ability to perform a task, whether it is chairing a meeting, making a presentation, getting dinner ready – or winning an Olympic medal.

Simple things such as loosening clothing and practising breathing techniques can help, or there are the various types of yoga designed to relax body and mind. Meditation, traditionally used to enhance spiritual growth, is now widely used as a means of escape from the hassles of day-to-day life. Massage, either in the form of a vigorous deep muscle massage or in a gentler aromatherapy type massage, can greatly affect your physical and mental state.

When I competed, before my warm-up I would often find the quietest spot I could and calmly sit and think about the coming hours. Whilst I did this I would consciously relax my breathing using a technique I had learnt doing yoga known as 'dragon breath', or ujjayi. 'Ujjayi breathing' translates as 'victorious breathing'. The air is drawn in through both nostrils and the glottis is held partially closed. I found this technique particularly relaxing and it helped me to both relax and focus.

RELAX

A relaxation technique I was taught several years ago has been an integral part of some of my best performances in the pool. 'Relaxation' is perhaps a bit misguiding, as I found the technique would calm me down if I was feeling anxious about a race, but I could also use it to get geared up for a performance if I was too relaxed. A better term would be 'focusing'.

It is not something you can do while driving, doing the ironing or something else. You have to devote yourself to this one task – it should only take ten minutes or so.

The first thing to do is choose a piece of music you like that has a very slow tempo and is tranquil. Put the music on and find a darkened room with somewhere comfortable to lie down. Remove your shoes. Lie motionless for a minute or two and then point your toes like a ballet dancer, hold for 20–30 seconds and relax. Then clench your fists as tight as they will possibly go, again for 20–30 seconds and relax. Take a short break before pushing your stomach out using your diaphragm, push until you feel like you are about to burst. Do this for the same time as the previous two tasks and relax. Next, do all three simultaneously again for 20–30 seconds. This should by now have you very relaxed physically.

The next part is working on your mind and is very simple. Imagine yourself in your favourite place – mine was always on a beach – and that in this place you have no physical weight. For example, I would always imagine I could feel that the sand was warm and soft under my feet yet at the same time I did not sink into it nor leave any footprints. The key to this part is to let your imagination run a 'serene riot' without letting yourself fall asleep; remember the point is to focus yourself. After about three or so minutes of maintaining this state you should open your eyes, get up in a controlled manner, hopefully feeling focused and precise, and also relaxed.

Giles Long
Paralympic swimmer

OVERCOMING RESISTANCE

Not everybody is receptive to trying out ideas such as these. Some people feel too self-conscious, or they are sceptical or stubborn. They like to do it their own way.

I've been like that in the past. Some of these and other techniques do sound a little strange but, if you want to get an edge – to get that little extra – you need to try the orthodox and the unorthodox. You have to be open to new ideas, especially when the people who are using them are so successful. So why not import some of them into your daily life? Here's a checklist:

- Eliminate negative self-talk and affirmations. Stick to the positive.
- Don't become too reliant on any particular technique. They are supporting your ability and are not enough on their own.
- Choose the techniques that suit you and drop the ones that don't.

And finally, although these techniques can and should be part of your performance toolbox, remember there is a right time and place for each of them. Occasionally you will meet people who are obsessed with such tools, sometimes to the extent that it seems that they are opting out of everyday life. These people are no longer just using the tools – they are trapped in the toolbox.

AFTERWORD

A call to arms

IF ONLY

My most powerful motivation technique, the one that took me to NZ, and then took me away again seven years later on the yachts, and the one that drives me to stay in the UK now no matter how hard it currently feels is: 'If only'. I envisage myself at the age of 70 in my rocking chair, smoking a pipe (I hope to smoke a pipe!) reflecting back on my life, and thinking: 'If only I had tried this or that …'

I like to fail, for it means that at least I have had a go, and if in giving it a go I succeed then so much the better, and if I fail then at least I will not be there in my rocking chair thinking: 'If only…'

Matt Heath
Yachtsman

What is the worst thing you could say whilst lying on your death bed? There are two that I would like to try and avoid and they are, in no particular order, 'I wish I had …' and 'I could have, but …'.

I constantly meet people who say these two things. The first one I just find sad – I can empathize with it. The people who say this often haven't been able to be brave when it came to grasping their dream. More often then not, they have taken the comfortable option in life as opposed to the one they wanted. The thing they desired has seemed untouchable – too difficult to achieve. They feel they would have to put too much on the line. But it haunts them.

The second tends to be someone who has little understanding of what it really takes to achieve their 'could have' fantasy.

Once a week, I will meet someone who says, 'I could have gone to the Olympics.' Being the person I am, I smile and say, 'Oh really? What sport?' and hold a pleasant conversation with them about how talented they were but, but, but, but … What I really want to say – and I probably will one day when I am feeling tired and grumpy – is, 'Look – if you could have been, you would have been. It's as simple as that.'

There is so much more to being an Olympic athlete than simply having a modicum of ability. You have to be motivated, be able to set goals and work towards them, and make sacrifices and live with them. You tread the path that is seldom trod.

To say 'I could have rowed in the Olympics but then I discovered women and beer' is absolutely crazy. The same types of people sometimes offer similar excuse for other aspects of their lives. 'Oh, I would do some exercise, but I simply don't have the time.' 'I would spend more time with the kids, but work is so hectic.'

I'm often asked now, 'Would you trade in your current life in return for having two legs again?'

The answer? 'No, absolutely not.'

What I have gained has far exceeded what I have lost.

So if you take anything from this book, let it be this: a desire to live your life to the full, the inspiration to be the best you can be, the determination to strive to constantly improve and, above all, the courage to live your life without regret.

Contributors

Jeanie Baker has been an accredited sports dietician since 1992 and works mostly with teams but also some individuals. She currently advises Scunthorpe United FC and the Lucozade Sport Science Academy. In the past she has worked with the Paralympic and Olympic Great Britain swimming teams, Castleford Rugby League, Hull City FC, Barnsley FC and Halifax Town FC.

Richard Cullen is head of HR for the National Probation Service. Until 2001 he was a serving police officer in the Metropolitan Police Service, retiring as a Commander and the Met's Director of Training and Development. He has extensive experience of policing major events and disorder. He lectures and writes extensively on leadership and the management of change.

Richard Davies is the CEO for ATP Properties, responsible for all the commercial activity of the men's professional tennis tour.

William Deeley is the managing director and founder of the Tythe Barn in Launton. The Tythe Barn is now considered one of the premier wedding and conference venues in Oxfordshire.

John Dunne was the one of first climbers to combine world-class sport fitness and strength, and then apply these attributes to extreme climbing situations. Previously, climbers tended to be very bold or very fit, but seldom both. In the late '80s and mid-'90s, John established some of the toughest sport and traditional climbs in the world.

Tim Eden was formerly the professor of paediatric oncology at the University of Manchester and the Christie Hospital. He is now the Teenage Cancer Trust's Professor of Teenage Cancer Medicine.

Donna Fraser is a three-time Olympian. She won a silver and two bronze medals at the 1998 Commonwealth Games in Kuala Lumpur, and bronze medals at both the indoor and outdoor European Athletics Championships as part of the British 4×400m relay team.

Lesley Garside was trained at the Royal Military Academy Sandhurst, where she founded and captained the first women's rugby team in the Army. Following a successful career in the Royal Logistic Corps, Lesley began a second career in business. Initially focusing on the project management of software implementation, she then completed an MSc in management sciences and moved into the world of operations. Lesley is currently the Operations Director for Northgate Public Services.

Ali Gill is a triple-Olympic oarswoman and now managing director of Getfeedback, a company that is in the business of talent management and development. She is author of *The Yanks at Oxford,* a tale of mismanagement in the Oxford and Cambridge Boat Race, and a public speaker on the topic of organizational development.

Matthew Heath is a professional yachtsman employed as first mate in the super yacht industry. He has been responsible for the safe passage across the Atlantic of yachts valued in excess of $10 million.

Lars Humer is currently Head Coach for British disability swimming. As an athlete, Lars was three-time New Zealand Surf Ironman Champion and New Zealand team captain, and competed on the gruelling professional Ironman Circuit in Australia. In the dual role of assistant coach and team manager of the New Zealand Surf Life Saving team, he guided the team to victory at the 1998 World Championships, beating Australia for the first time in 40 years.

Kumar Kamalagharan is managing director of Fruit Pie Music. He has worked with hundreds of bands and has tour-managed Steve Winwood, Frou Frou, Imogen Heap (solo), Dum Dums, Damage, Beverley Knight, Tom Jones' UK band and Razorlight. His work includes tour, production and logistics management, including pre-tour planning, budgeting and accountancy.

Georgina Lee is a retired British Olympian. She swam in the 2000 and 2004 Olympic Games, as well as multiple Commonwealth, World and European Championships. An Olympic finalist, Commonwealth champion and European medallist, Georgina currently holds four British records. She now works as a forensic and litigation consultant in Dallas, Texas.

Giles Long is a triple-Paralympic gold medal winning swimmer and current world record holder. He delivers motivational speeches to children, encouraging them to participate in sport, and to businesses to help them embrace change. He is also a member of the British Athletes Commission.

Petra Markell studied fine art in London and is now partner in an interior design and decorating company.

Sheelagh Rodgers is Head of Clinical Psychology in NHS Highlands. She currently works with UK Athletics and the English Institute of Sport as a Clinical and Sports Psychologist. She attended the 1996 and 2004 Olympic Games as the HQ psychologist for the British Olympic Association, and the 2000 Paralympics as psychologist with the swimming team.

Richard Shaw is a teenage cancer survivor and is a trustee of the Teenage Cancer Trust. He has over 30 years' business experience and has held senior management and director roles for over 18 of them.

David Thomas is the highest-rated of only two International Grandmasters of Memory in the US. He is a World Memory Championship medallist and holds a current memory world record. His book *Essential Lifeskills: Improving Your Memory* is a global bestseller.

Etienne de Villiers was the former president of Disney TV for Europe, Africa and the Middle East. He has served on a number of corporate boards, including ITV, and is a founding partner of Englefield Capital, a billion-dollar private equity fund. He is also the chairman of the Association of Tennis Professionals.

Index